Becoming Stoic

The Essential Lessons

Rand Cardwell

For the Beijing Crew:
JB, Matt, Erick, and Josh

Contents

Becoming Stoic Website	ix
Preface	xi
Chapter 1	**1**
CLARITY	
Determining What You Can Control	3
Focusing on Control	7
Learning to Say "No"	9
Accept What You Can't Control	11
Adjusting Goals	13
Chapter 2	**17**
EMOTIONS	
Control and Anger	19
Remaining Calm	23
Maintaining Self-Control	27
Happy and Content	29
Inner Stability	31
Chapter 3	**35**
AWARENESS	
Life Worth Living	37
Seeing Your True Self	41
Striving for Improvement	43
True Freedom	47
Opinions of Others	51
Chapter 4	**55**
UNBIASED THOUGHT	
Master of Your Mind	57
On Making Hasty Decisions	59
Focusing on Self-Improvement	63
A Mental Fortress	67
Committment to Being Rational	71
Chapter 5	**75**
RIGHT ACTION	

Being Recognized as a Stoic	77
Doing the Right Thing	81
Put it to Practice	85
Daily Improvement	89
Focusing on Now	93
Chapter 6	97
PROBLEM SOLVING	
Seeing It For What It Is	99
Adjusting Course	101
Mental Resilience	105
Forgiving Yourself	109
Proper Prior Planning	113
Chapter 7	117
DUTY	
Making A Difficult Decision	119
Receiving the Will of the Universe	123
Being Honorable, Regardless	127
Doing What You Love	131
Your Duty to Lead	135
Chapter 8	139
PRAGMATISM	
Not Caving to Obstacles	141
Doing What is Necessary	145
Life Like a Warrior	149
Pick Your Battles	153
Wisdom from Any Source	157
Chapter 9	161
FORTITUDE and RESILIENCE	
Face It Fearlessly	163
It All Makes Me Stronger	167
Training for Crisis	171
Mentally Solid	175
Strong At All Times	179
Chapter 10	183
VIRTUE and KINDNESS	
Let Them Shine	185
Good for the Whole	189
Giving Back Love	193
The Higher Standard	197

Focus on Correcting Self	201
Chapter 11	205
ACCEPTANCE	
Facing The Changes	207
Change: The Constant of the Universe	211
Accepting Change	215
Go With the Flow	219
I'll Be Okay	223
Chapter 12	227
MEDITATION ON MORTALITY	
Today Could Be Your Last	229
What Do You Own?	233
No Fear	237
Motivated Living	241
Your Last Day?	245
About the Author	249
Also by Rand Cardwell	251

Becoming Stoic: The Essential Lessons

Sixty core teachings on Perception, Action, and Will

First Edition

Copyright © 2025 by Rand Cardwell

Al rights reserved. No part of this book may be reproduced, stored in a retrieval system, or transmitted in any form or by any means, without the prior written permission of the publisher, except in the case of brief quotations embedded in critical articles or reviews.

The information contained in this book is sold without warranty, either expressed or implied. Neither the author, publisher, dealers, and distributors will be held liable for any damages caused or alleged to be caused directly or indirectly by this book.

First published: November 2025

Imprint: Published by Rand Cardwell

Editing: Bhavana Patel

Cover Photo: Freepik

ISBN: 978-1-7374719-1-2

Becoming Stoic Website

Check out the *becoming stoic* website to find additional tools on your journey to fine tuning yourself into the best that you can be. We can also be found on Facebook, Instagram, and X.

www.becomingstoic.net

Preface

This book began as a return—back through pages already written, truths already uncovered, and lessons already lived.

Becoming Stoic: The Essential Lessons draws from the three foundational works in the *Becoming Stoic* series: *Lessons on Perception, Lessons on Action,* and *Lessons on Will*. Each of those volumes was a focused meditation on a core discipline of Stoic philosophy. This edition is something different. It is not a replacement—it is a refinement. Within these pages are sixty carefully chosen lessons: twenty from each original book, selected for their clarity, practicality, and enduring value.

These are the lessons I've found myself returning to most often. They are reminders I've written not only for others, but for myself. And though they are brief, they are not shallow. Each one is a stepping stone across the ever-moving current of life—a chance to pause, reflect, and reorient yourself toward the kind of person you are striving to become.

Stoicism does not promise perfection. It does not erase struggle. What it offers is a way to meet the world with honesty and strength—to see clearly, act wisely, and endure well. If the full trilogy repre-

Preface

sents a journey of transformation, this book is a traveling companion: light to carry, easy to reference, and grounded in practice.

If you find value in the lessons shared here, I invite you to explore the full Becoming Stoic series. Each volume offers deeper reflections and practical exercises rooted in the discipline of daily growth—whether you are learning to sharpen your perception, guide your actions, or strengthen your will.

Whether you are new to Stoicism or returning for a reminder, may these words serve you as they have served me—quietly, steadily, and with purpose.

— *Rand Cardwell*

Chapter 1
CLARITY

Determining What You Can Control

"I will determine what I can change and what I cannot."

* * *

Our first lesson is on the importance of focusing on what is within our control and letting go of what is not. It is at the core of Stoic philosophy and should be your focus as you start your Stoic journey. Stoics believe that many of the problems we face in life stem from our tendency to try to control things that are outside of our control. By fixating on things we cannot change, we waste our energy and create unnecessary stress and frustration for ourselves.

To determine what we can change and what we cannot, a Stoic would begin by focusing on their own attitudes and behaviors. They would try to develop self-control, knowing that they couldn't change what happened to them, but they could change how they responded to it.

A Stoic would also strive to develop the virtue of wisdom by

Becoming Stoic

attempting to see things impartially and without succumbing to bias or emotion. By focusing on what is within their control, they can avoid getting caught up in the chaos and confusion of the outside world.

At the same time, a Stoic would recognize that there are many things in life that are outside of our control. For example, we cannot control the weather, other people's attitudes, or unexpected events. By accepting these things as they are, and focusing on what we can control, we can reduce our stress and anxiety, and approach life with greater clarity and purpose.

This does not mean, however, that a Stoic should simply resign themselves to fate. Rather, they would seek to take deliberate action to improve their situation, wherever possible. This might involve identifying areas where they can make a difference, and focusing their energy and attention on those things.

For example, if facing a difficult situation, a Stoic might ask themselves, "What can I do to improve this situation?" If they cannot change the situation itself, they might focus on changing their own attitude or perspective. By looking at the situation in a more positive way, they can feel less stressed and anxious and handle it with more calm.

In the end, a Stoic tries to find inner peace and freedom by figuring out what they can change and what they can't. This allows them to maintain a sense of dignity, purpose, and fulfillment, regardless of what is happening in the world around them.

In practical terms, this might mean taking deliberate steps to manage stress and anxiety. For example, a Stoic might practice mindfulness meditation, seek the support of friends and family, or engage in physical exercise to release tension. They might also seek out opportunities for personal growth and learning, recognizing that challenges offer opportunities for self-improvement.

From a Stoic point of view, figuring out what we can change and what we can't is a great way to build inner strength, resilience, and

Determining What You Can Control

equanimity. By focusing on what is within our control, and letting go of what is not, we can approach life's challenges with greater clarity and purpose while maintaining a sense of inner peace and freedom.

Focusing on Control

"I will focus my actions on what I have control."

* * *

The philosophy of the Stoics was to concentrate on what we could control rather than worry about the things we could not. They held the opinion that some aspects of life are beyond our control, including the weather, other people's behavior, and even our own mental and physical health. On the other hand, they thought that some things, including our thoughts, attitudes, and behaviors, were under our control.

Focusing on what we can control is a hallmark of the stoic philosophy of life. We may avoid wasting time and energy on things that are out of our control by making an effort to focus our attention and energy on the things that we can control. As students, we have control over things like how much we study, how efficiently we arrange our notes, and how focused we are during an exam. We have no control over the level of difficulty of the exam questions, the conduct of our fellow students, or the professor's evaluation of us.

Becoming Stoic

We should not worry about things that are beyond our control, like the difficulty of the exam questions or the conduct of our classmates, a Stoic might suggest. Instead, we should focus on things we can change, like how well we study, how prepared we are, and how focused we are during the test.

We can live a more calm and contented life, free from pointless tension and worry, by concentrating on what is within our control. We don't have to let outside things get to us. Instead, we can focus on our own thoughts, attitudes, and actions.

We must exercise self-control and intelligence if we want to develop a Stoic philosophy of life. Self-control enables us to manage our own responses to outside events and to keep our composure in the face of difficulty. Being wise enables us to view situations objectively and shields us from prejudice or emotion.

A Stoic also understands that, despite some things being out of our control, we still have some control over them. The weather may not be something we can influence, but we can be ready for it by dressing appropriately and taking the essential safety measures. Even though we may not have any control over what other people do, we do have power over how we respond to them and the way we choose to engage with them.

Accepting what is beyond our control does not mean giving up on ourselves. Instead, we ought to make conscious efforts to make our condition better whenever possible. We can decide which problems we can solve and concentrate our efforts and attention there.

In conclusion, a stoic philosophy of life emphasizes focusing our attention on what we can manage. We may lead happier, more contented lives free from pointless stress and worry by focusing our attention and energy on the things we can control. This calls for developing self-discipline and intelligence, realizing the extent of our control over external events, and acting purposefully to better our circumstances whenever possible. We can face life's issues with better clarity and purpose while preserving a sense of inner freedom by adhering to these ideals.

Learning to Say "No"

"I will learn to say "no" to things that do not matter to me."

* * *

Stoicism has stood the test of time because it helps people figure out how to live a happier, more meaningful life. One of the fundamental principles of stoicism is to focus on what we can control and let go of what we cannot. This principle reminds us to focus our time and energy on things that are in line with our beliefs and goals. We should not waste our time and resources on things that are beyond our control or do not matter to us.

In this context, saying "no" to things that do not matter to us becomes crucial. It helps us put our goals and values in order of importance and avoid distractions and temptations that could take us off track. Saying "no" means making a conscious choice to stay focused on what is important in life. It is a form of self-control and self-discipline that helps us build inner strength and resilience.

When we say "no" to things that do not matter to us, we set

ourselves free from the burden of external expectations and social pressures. By living in line with our values and principles, we become more real and true to ourselves. This connection between our inner selves and the things we do gives us a sense of satisfaction and happiness that we can't get from chasing external goals that don't fit with our beliefs.

Moreover, saying "no" to things that do not matter to us helps us cultivate a stoic mindset that values reason, logic, and wisdom. It allows us to differentiate between what is essential and what is trivial, to focus on the present moment, and make the most of it. We learn to accept the things we cannot change and take responsibility for the things we can control. We become more able to handle problems and setbacks because we know we have the strength to get through them.

Finally, saying "no" to things that do not matter to us empowers us to create the life we want instead of being passive recipients of external circumstances. We become the creators of our own lives, putting together a plan that fits with our deepest values and goals. We become more proactive and intentional, taking ownership of our actions and decisions.

In conclusion, stoicism teaches us the importance of saying "no" to things that do not matter to us. It's a conscious choice to pay attention to what's important in life and live by our values and principles. Saying "no" helps us put our goals in order of importance, avoid distractions and temptations, and build inner strength and resilience. It is a form of self-control and self-discipline that leads to a more fulfilling and meaningful life. It's not what happens to you, but how you react to it that matters. Saying "no" to things that do not matter to us is a way to control our reactions and create the life we want.

Accept What You Can't Control

"I will accept what is beyond my ability to control."

* * *

Stoicism's fundamental goal is to help people learn how to be calm and strong internally, even when life gets tough. This philosophy is based on the belief that the only things we can control in life are our thoughts, beliefs, and actions. Everything else, including outside situations and events, is beyond our control. As a result, it is essential that we focus our efforts and energy on the things we can control and accept the things we cannot.

One of the primary teachings of Stoicism is that we should release ourselves from the worry and stress that come with attempting to change things that are out of our control. This doesn't mean that we should just sit back and do nothing when bad things happen. Instead, we should recognize that events themselves do not determine how we react to them. We have the power to choose our response to events and situations, regardless of their nature.

Stoicism says that when we accept things we can't change, we

Becoming Stoic

become stronger and more flexible. We can focus our efforts on cultivating our inner virtues, which are under our control and can make it easier for us to deal with life's ups and downs. These virtues include wisdom, courage, and compassion.

Wisdom is one of the primary virtues in Stoicism. It is the ability to make sound judgments and decisions in life. According to Stoicism, wisdom can be developed through experience and contemplation. The wise person recognizes the limits of their power and understands the impermanence of life. They accept what is beyond their control and focus their energy on improving themselves.

Courage is another crucial virtue in Stoicism. It is the ability to face difficulties and challenges with bravery and resilience. In Stoicism, courage is not the absence of fear but the willingness to act in the face of it. The courageous person recognizes that life is unpredictable and full of uncertainty, but they do not allow fear to paralyze them. Instead, they face their fears head-on and persevere through adversity.

Compassion is the third virtue in Stoicism. It is the ability to empathize with others and show kindness and understanding. In Stoicism, compassion is not an emotion but a way of life. The compassionate person recognizes that we are all connected and that we all share in the human experience. They treat others with respect and kindness, even in the face of adversity.

In conclusion, the Stoic philosophy teaches us to accept things that are out of our control by recognizing the limits of our power and focusing on improving ourselves instead of trying to change things that are beyond our control. When we accept what is beyond our control, we can become more resilient, keep our minds calm, and feel better. By developing the virtues of wisdom, courage, and kindness, we can deal with life's problems more easily and adapt to them. Stoicism gives us a practical plan for how to live a happy life, even when bad things happen.

Adjusting Goals

"I will avoid distractions and make adjustments to my goals."

* * *

According to the Stoics, the most important thing in life is to seek wisdom and virtue, even though there will be distractions and problems along the way. Instead of trying to get rid of these problems, the best way to reach your goals is to work hard and keep your attention on what's really important. In this situation, the statement "I will avoid distractions and make adjustments to my goal," supports the Stoic idea that one should avoid distractions and make changes to their goals.

The Stoics thought that the mind can win over events if it exercises self-control and uses reason to think about them. They talked about how important it is to have inner strength so that you can handle life's hard times without giving up. The hard mental training that leads to resilience includes developing virtue, thinking about yourself over and over again, and getting a clear sense of what you want to do with your life.

Stoics thought that chasing after pleasure was a temporary and ultimately unsatisfying goal. It was one of the most common things they told people not to do. They told people to focus instead on developing moral qualities like wisdom, courage, fairness, and self-control. These traits are the foundation of a fair and peaceful society, and they also lead to personal happiness.

The desire for fame or fortune was another diversion that the Stoics frowned upon. They believed that a person's moral worth should be based more on their inner qualities than their outward successes and that outward success was not a reliable predictor of moral worth or personal satisfaction. The Stoics advised people to put their attention on honing their inner traits rather than pursuing worldly success.

This doesn't mean, though, that the Stoics didn't want people to have goals or try to be successful on the outside. Instead, they thought that having a sense of direction and purpose was crucial for leading a fulfilling life. They talked about how important it is to change your goals as your situation changes. They did this because they knew that things could change and new problems could arise.

In this way, the statement, "I will avoid distractions and make adjustments to my goal," exemplifies the Stoic principle of adjusting to changing circumstances without straying from one's purpose. The Stoics thought that a person's sense of purpose should be strong enough to withstand distractions and pressures from the outside but also flexible enough to deal with new problems and opportunities.

To find this balance, the Stoics stressed how important it was to have goals that were both attainable and in line with one's values. They thought that a person's goals should be set by their inner values, not by rewards from the outside world. They also thought that a clear sense of purpose and a commitment to self-discipline should drive a person to reach their goals.

The Stoics told people to stay calm and logical in the face of

Adjusting Goals

distractions and problems from the outside world. They stressed how important it was to have a strong and resilient inner character because they thought that a person's ability to deal with problems outside of themselves depended a lot on how they thought about themselves.

Overall, the phrase, "I will avoid distractions and make adjustments to my goal," embodies the Stoic philosophy of avoiding distractions and changing one's goals. To pursue wisdom and virtue, you need to be disciplined, think about yourself, and have a clear goal. Stopping distractions and focusing on what's really important can help us deal with outside problems and reach our goals while staying true to who we are on the inside.

Chapter 2
EMOTIONS

Control and Anger

"I will control myself and not become angry at others."

* * *

Stoicism has provided a framework for many people to live their lives and make sense of the world around them. One of the most important lessons of Stoicism is that we can't change what happens to us, but we can change how we react to it. This means that we have the power to choose how we react to the things that happen to us. By practicing self-control, we can find peace and happiness within ourselves, even when things are hard.

The Stoics believed that we should not be attached to external things such as wealth, fame, or status. They argued that these things are transient and ultimately do not bring us lasting happiness. Instead, they advised us to focus on developing our character and cultivating inner virtues such as wisdom, courage, and justice. This requires us to take responsibility for our own actions and be mindful of our thoughts and emotions.

Becoming Stoic

In the case of anger, the Stoics believed that it is an irrational and destructive emotion that arises when we hold unrealistic expectations for or demands on others. They taught that anger arises from our own beliefs and judgments rather than from external events themselves. Therefore, we have the power to change our beliefs and judgments and thereby control our anger.

One of the techniques that the Stoics used to control their emotions was mindfulness. By being aware of our thoughts and emotions, we can catch ourselves before we become angry and choose a more rational and constructive response. We can also reflect on our beliefs and values and strive to align them with Stoic ideals.

For example, if we believe that people should always behave in a certain way, we are likely to become angry when they do not meet our expectations. However, if we reflect on our beliefs and values, we may realize that our expectations are unrealistic and that people have the freedom to behave as they choose. This can help us let go of our anger and focus on more constructive ways of dealing with the situation.

Another technique that the Stoics used to control their emotions was reflection. By reflecting on our beliefs and values, we can gain a deeper understanding of ourselves and our place in the world. We can also strive to align our actions with our values and virtues, which can bring us a sense of fulfillment and inner peace.

Ultimately, the Stoics believed that self-control and inner peace were essential for living a fulfilling life. By mastering our emotions and reactions, we can live in harmony with ourselves and others and achieve a state of tranquility and contentment. This requires us to take responsibility for our own actions and be mindful of our thoughts and emotions. It also requires us to reflect on our beliefs and values and strive to align them with Stoic ideals.

In the end, Stoicism teaches us that we can't change what happens to us, but we can change how we react to it. By practicing self-control, we can find peace and happiness within ourselves, even when things are hard. The Stoics thought that anger is a harmful

Control and Anger

emotion that comes from our own thoughts and beliefs. To control our anger, we need to practice mindfulness and reflection and strive to align our beliefs and values with Stoic ideals. Ultimately, self-control and inner peace are essential for living a fulfilling life and can help us achieve a state of tranquility and contentment.

Remaining Calm

"**I will remain calm and not allow myself to become overly emotional.**"

* * *

The philosophy of Stoicism has been widely recognized for its practical approach to life. One of the core principles of Stoicism is the belief that emotions, especially negative ones like anger, fear, and sadness, can cloud our judgment and prevent us from acting rationally. As such, it is essential to cultivate emotional detachment or indifference towards external events and circumstances.

The Stoics believed that emotions could be controlled, and it is essential to recognize that emotions do not have to control us. In this sense, it is possible to have a positive attitude, regardless of the circumstances. When you can control your emotions, you can stay calm and not get too emotional, even when things are hard or stressful. This way, one can develop emotional resilience and be less affected by negative events.

One technique that Stoics often recommend for emotional

Becoming Stoic

control is negative visualization. Negative visualization involves imagining the worst-case scenario in a given situation and mentally preparing oneself for it. The idea is to prepare oneself for the worst so that if it does happen, one is not caught off guard, and if it does not happen, one is pleasantly surprised. Negative visualization helps one develop emotional resilience and be less affected by negative events.

Self-reflection and self-awareness are also essential techniques that Stoics recommend to cultivate emotional detachment. By observing their own emotional responses and seeking to understand the underlying beliefs and assumptions that are driving them, one can gain greater control over their emotions and respond to situations in a more rational and balanced way.

In Stoic philosophy, it's not enough to just hide your feelings; you also need to find peace and calm inside yourself, no matter what's going on outside. By staying calm and not letting your emotions get the best of you, you can develop this sense of inner harmony and live a more meaningful life. This goal requires a lot of self-discipline and the willingness to face hard situations with calmness and strength.

Some people might think that the idea of emotional detachment is cold or heartless, but Stoics don't want people to live without any feelings at all. Emotions are an essential part of being human, and they can provide valuable information about the world around us. However, it is important to recognize that emotions can also be irrational and impulsive. We can harness the power of our emotions and use them to our advantage rather than allowing them to control us.

Stoics also believe that we should focus on what is within our control and not worry about what is outside of it. This way, we can avoid unnecessary stress and anxiety and focus on the things that we can change. This method is also in line with the idea of emotional detachment, since it encourages us to let go of our attachment to events and situations outside of ourselves.

In conclusion, Stoic philosophy offers a practical way to control your emotions and become less attached to them. By practicing emotional detachment, we can stay calm and logical in difficult or

Remaining Calm

stressful situations, build emotional strength, and live a more satisfying and meaningful life. Negative visualization, self-reflection, and self-awareness are important tools that can help us reach this goal. While emotional detachment may seem cold or heartless to some, it is an essential aspect of emotional control that can help us live a more balanced and fulfilling life.

Maintaining Self-Control

"I will maintain self-control in all aspects of my life."

* * *

Stoicism is based on the idea that people should try to keep control of themselves in all parts of their lives and not let their feelings or outside circumstances tell them what to do. To a Stoic, self-control is not just about personal discipline but about living a life of integrity, compassion, and wisdom.

One of the key tenets of Stoicism is the notion that individuals should focus on what they can control rather than become overwhelmed by things that are outside of their control. For example, a Stoic should avoid getting angry or frustrated about traffic or the weather since these things are beyond their control. Instead, they should focus on their own thoughts, attitudes, and actions and strive to act in a rational and ethical way.

Maintaining self-control requires a high level of self-awareness and mindfulness. A Stoic should be aware of their own views and values and be able to identify when their emotions or impulses are starting to take over. By recognizing these moments, a Stoic can take steps to regain control of their thoughts and actions and avoid making decisions that they may later regret.

In practice, self-control may involve setting clear goals and developing healthy routines. A Stoic might set a goal to exercise regularly, eat a healthy diet, or practice mindfulness meditation. By establishing these routines, a Stoic can build self-discipline and avoid succumbing to impulsive or unhealthy behaviors.

Self-control also requires being mindful of one's own urges and desires. A Stoic should be able to recognize when they are feeling tempted to engage in risky or addictive behaviors and take steps to resist these urges. This might involve developing strategies to avoid triggers or seeking support from friends or family members.

Accepting what you can't change or control may be one of the hardest parts of being in charge of yourself. A Stoic should recognize that there are many things in life that are beyond their control, such as natural disasters, illness, or the actions of others. By accepting these things, a Stoic can avoid becoming consumed by anger or frustration and instead focus on the things that they can control.

Ultimately, maintaining self-control is about living a life of integrity and compassion. A Stoic should strive to act in an honest and reasonable way and avoid acting in ways that might harm others. By doing so, they can contribute to the greater good of society as a whole.

In conclusion, self-control is a crucial component of Stoicism and involves focusing on what can be controlled while accepting what cannot. It requires self-awareness, mindfulness, and discipline and involves setting clear goals, developing healthy routines, and resisting urges and desires. For a Stoic, maintaining self-control is not just a personal discipline but a way of living a life of integrity, compassion, and wisdom. By cultivating a sense of inner peace and contentment, a Stoic can contribute to the greater good of society and inspire others to follow their example.

Happy and Content

"I will be happy and content with what I have."

* * *

The Stoic philosophy holds that true happiness is not derived from external circumstances or material possessions but rather from one's own inner state of mind. This reflects a core principle of the philosophy, which is that external events and circumstances are beyond our control. Instead, we should focus on cultivating a state of inner tranquility and contentment by accepting the things we cannot change and focusing our efforts on what we can control—our own thoughts, attitudes, and actions.

The Stoics believed that the key to a fulfilling life is not in pursuing external objects but in living according to reason, virtue, and wisdom. The pursuit of external objects, such as wealth, fame, or power, is futile, as they are outside of our control and subject to change. Instead, the Stoics encouraged us to focus on developing our inner selves, to cultivate wisdom, and to live in accordance with our own nature.

Becoming Stoic

The Stoics said that the best way to find inner peace was to accept our circumstances and pay attention to the present moment. This means being happy with what we already have and learning to be grateful and appreciative for it. By doing so, we can reduce anxiety, stress, and dissatisfaction and find a greater sense of peace and fulfillment in our lives.

One of the ways in which the Stoics emphasized the importance of focusing on the present moment was through the practice of mindfulness. Mindfulness involves paying attention to the present moment without judgment and with an open and accepting attitude. By practicing mindfulness, we can become more aware of our thoughts, emotions, and physical sensations and learn to accept them as they are without reacting to them or trying to change them.

Self-control was another way the Stoics stressed the importance of finding inner peace. Self-control involves being aware of our desires and impulses and learning to control them through reason and discipline. By doing so, we can avoid being controlled by our emotions and impulses and instead live in accordance with our own nature.

The Stoics also thought that the only way to be truly happy is to live in line with our own nature. This involves living a life of virtue, wisdom, and reason. Virtue involves living in accordance with the highest values of humanity, such as honesty, integrity, compassion, and courage. Wisdom involves using reason to guide our actions and decisions and to cultivate an understanding of the nature of reality. Reason involves using our rational faculties to understand the world around us and to live in accordance with our own nature.

In conclusion, the Stoic philosophy teaches us that true happiness is not found in external circumstances but in our own minds. By cultivating inner tranquility, accepting our circumstances, and focusing on the present moment, we can find a greater sense of peace and fulfillment in our lives. This involves being content with what we have, cultivating a sense of gratitude and appreciation, and living in accordance with reason, virtue, and wisdom. By doing so, we can live a fulfilling life and find true happiness and contentment.

Inner Stability

"I will remain stable to events that others find passionate."

* * *

One of the most important ideas in Stoicism is the idea of inner stability and resilience. This means developing a way of thinking that helps you stay calm and logical in the face of challenging or emotionally charged events outside of yourself. The Stoics thought that passion or strong emotions caused trouble and turmoil, so they encouraged people to develop a rational, logical way of thinking that could help them feel calm and balanced inside. This doesn't mean that Stoics were completely against feeling or emotion, though, because they knew that emotions are a natural and necessary part of being human. But they thought that training and discipline could help a person gain some control over his or her emotions.

The Stoics thought that emotional detachment was a key part of being strong and stable on the inside. By practicing emotional detachment, you can learn to react less to outside events and more thought-

Becoming Stoic

fully and rationally to them. This can help you feel more at peace with yourself and live a fuller life, free from the constant upheaval of strong emotions and passions.

To the Stoics, the key to emotional detachment was to focus on what one could control and let go of what one could not control. They thought that many of our feelings come from caring too much about things we can't change, like what other people think, the weather, or what other people do. By recognizing that we have no control over these things, we can learn to let go of our attachment to them and focus on what we can control, which is our own thoughts, feelings, and actions.

In practice, this means learning to accept what happens to us without judgment or resistance and instead focusing on our response to the situation. Rather than allowing external events to determine our emotional state, we can choose to respond in a calm and rational manner that is in line with our values and goals.

The Stoics also thought that it takes constant practice and discipline to build inner stability and resilience. This means that we need to be intentional about our thoughts, feelings, and actions and work to cultivate a mindset that is focused on what we can control rather than what we cannot. This takes a certain amount of self-awareness and introspection, because we need to be able to tell when we're getting too attached to things outside of ourselves and turn our attention back to the things we can control.

The Stoics also stressed the importance of being in the present moment and thinking about yourself. By practicing mindfulness, we can learn to be more present in the moment and less distracted by our thoughts and emotions. This can help us feel more peaceful and calm on the inside, even when things are hard or challenging.

Self-reflection, on the other hand, involves taking the time to reflect on our thoughts, feelings, and actions and to assess whether they are in line with our values and goals. This can help us figure out where we might be too attached to things outside of ourselves or where our feelings might be getting the best of us. We can continue

Inner Stability

to build inner stability and strength over time by being honest with ourselves and making changes as needed.

In conclusion, Stoicism is based on the idea of inner stability and resilience. It stresses how important it is to develop a mindset that allows us to stay calm and rational in the face of outside events, no matter how difficult or emotionally charged they may be. By practicing emotional detachment, mindfulness, and self-reflection, we can learn to react less to outside events and more thoughtfully and rationally to them.

Chapter 3
AWARENESS

Life Worth Living

"I will live a life worth living."

* * *

Stoicism's core principle is the idea of living a life that is worthwhile. According to Stoicism, leading a life that is worth living means cultivating virtues and exercising self-control, wisdom, and courage regardless of external circumstances. This lesson will examine what it means to live a life that is worth living from a Stoic perspective and how we might put these principles into practice in our daily lives.

    The Stoics held that people are rational beings with the ability to think, analyze, and make decisions. They also thought that people could control their thoughts, feelings, and actions and that, no matter what was going on outside, people could find inner peace and happiness by practicing virtues and self-discipline. The Stoics placed a lot of importance on being smart, brave, fair, and in control of yourself. These qualities are viewed as means to leading a life that is worthwhile in addition to being desirable in and of themselves.

    According to the Stoic philosophy, leading a worthwhile life means following reason and virtue. This means having a firm grasp on what is genuinely important in life and aligning one's behaviors and intentions with these ideals. *Eudaimonia*, which can be translated as "happiness," "flourishing," or "fulfillment," is what the Stoics consider to be the ultimate end of human life. The modern idea of happiness as a subjective emotional state is not the same as the Stoic concept of *eudaimonia*, though. Instead, *eudaimonia* is a state of inner peace and satisfaction brought about by leading a life in accordance with one's principles and virtues.

The Stoics hold that one's ability to reach true happiness is not dependent on external factors like income, status, or health. Instead, it is important to consider one's own nature and character. Stoics held that regardless of external circumstances, one can cultivate virtues and practice self-control, knowledge, and resilience. This means that one may maintain composure, reason, and virtue even in the face of difficulty.

Stoics hold that in order to live a life that is worth living, one must accept responsibility for their own thoughts, emotions, and actions. This means realizing that one is in charge of their own thoughts and emotions and that their state of mind is independent of their environment. This means that rather than just reacting spontaneously, one may choose how to perceive and react to events in one's life.

A Stoic, for example, wouldn't give in to hopelessness or anger when things go wrong, like when they lose their job or their relationship ends. Instead, a Stoic would recognize that they can't change the situation and focus on what they can change, which is how they react to it. A Stoic would show self-control by not acting on impulse and instead choosing a response that is thought-out and based on principles.

The Stoics also believe that gaining wisdom is an important part of living a good life. Wisdom means knowing what is really important in life and making sure that your actions and goals are in line with these values. The Stoics believed that virtues like intelligence, courage, justice, and self-control were the most valuable things in life.

Life Worth Living

You can find inner peace and happiness that are unaffected by what's happening outside by adhering to these guidelines.

Stoics also emphasize the significance of developing resilience. The ability to face challenges and misfortune without losing one's sense of purpose or inner peace is known as resilience. Stoics hold that one can develop resilience by accepting that hardship is an unavoidable aspect of life and that one can choose how to handle it.

Seeing Your True Self

"I will see myself as I truly am."

* * *

A fundamental Stoic principle, self-knowledge, is reflected in the words, "I will see myself as I truly am." The Stoics thought that knowing oneself and one's place in the world was the key to living well. This required an open assessment of one's own thoughts, attitudes, and behaviors, as well as an acceptance of one's own knowledge and skill gaps. In this lesson, I'll look at Stoicism's idea of self-knowledge and talk about how it relates to modern life.

In Stoicism, self-knowledge is a process of self-examination that calls for honesty, introspection, and reflection. The Stoics held that everyone has the natural ability to reason and that this ability can be improved by studying philosophy. We can better understand ourselves and the world around us by using reason to analyze our own thoughts and emotions.

In Stoicism, mindfulness is one of the most important methods for self-knowledge. Mindfulness means paying attention to one's own thoughts and feelings without judgment or attachment. This kind of self-observation allows us to learn about our own thought and emotion processes. This can assist us in recognizing and overcoming unfavorable tendencies and biases, as well as in forming a more unbiased and logical worldview.

The understanding of our own limitations is a crucial component of Stoicism's self-knowledge. The Stoics held that while we should work to the utmost extent possible to enhance our logical faculties, we should equally acknowledge that our knowledge and skills have their limits. By avoiding overconfidence and arrogance and adopting a more open and inquisitive outlook on the world, this humility and self-awareness can assist us.

Living in harmony with nature was another principle highlighted by the Stoics. This required us to acknowledge our place in the natural world and make an effort to live in accordance with its natural laws. This meant accepting our own mortality and the transience of all things, as well as living in accordance with our own ideals and principles.

In Stoicism, self-knowledge can only be attained through a commitment to continual introspection and reflection. As we must face our own shortcomings and limitations, this may be a difficult and occasionally unpleasant process. The benefits of self-awareness, however, are enormous because they enable us to lead lives that are more purposeful and satisfying.

One of the main benefits of self-knowledge in Stoicism is that it helps people feel calm and peaceful inside. We can cultivate a more balanced and resilient attitude by learning more about who we are and the environment in which we live. This can help you deal with life's problems and uncertainties and keep your cool when things get tough.

Striving for Improvement

"I will focus on self-improvement in all aspects of my life."

* * *

Stoicism is based on the idea that the best way to live a happy life is to improve yourself. In all aspects of their lives, the Stoic philosophy encourages people to concentrate on their personal development. This means that people need to work on improving their connections with other people and their status in society, as well as their physical, mental, and emotional well-being.

Self-improvement is a lifetime path that calls for commitment, self-control, and a clear sense of direction. Stoic philosophy gives people a way to reach this goal by emphasizing the importance of logical reasoning, self-reflection, and self-discipline. The Stoics held that people should take charge of their own lives and actively try to better themselves rather than relying on events or circumstances outside of their control to determine their happiness and success.

Becoming Stoic

Stoicism says that one of the most important ways to improve yourself is to learn to control yourself and be disciplined. The Stoics thought that people must learn to control their impulses and emotions if they want to be peaceful and calm inside. People must practice mindfulness and self-awareness and think about their actions and decisions in order to figure out what they need to work on.

The development of virtues is a crucial component of Stoic self-improvement. The Stoics held that in order to lead a happy and satisfying life, people must work to acquire virtues like wisdom, courage, justice, and self-control. These qualities are regarded as crucial for one's own development as well as for creating deep and lasting connections with others.

Stoicism puts a lot of emphasis on one's own personal growth and development, as well as the importance of being a good citizen and taking care of your community. The Stoics held that each person had a responsibility to contribute to society's well-being and to work toward establishing a just and equitable society. This means that people have to be involved in their communities and work for the good of everyone.

The idea of *"amor fati,"* or "love of fate," is one of Stoicism's basic tenets. This means that humans must learn to accept and welcome whatever fate or circumstances they may experience and to use them as opportunities for growth and self-improvement. The Stoics held that instead of worrying about matters beyond their control, people should concentrate on what they can manage. By accepting and embracing their fate, individuals can develop a sense of inner peace and contentment, even in the face of tragedy.

Stoicism also emphasizes the value of attention and being present in the moment. The Stoics held that people should learn to concentrate on the here and now rather than obsessing over the past or worrying about the future. People can experience clarity and inner peace and live a much fuller and happier life by being aware and present in the moment.

Striving for Improvement

Being a Stoic is a journey, not a destination. It takes time and effort to transform how you see yourself, your thoughts and actions, and how you interact with others. Stoicism demands that you always work to better yourself in all aspects of your life. It is a never-ending process.

True Freedom

"I will not feel compelled, hindered, or limited in any way and will truly be free."

* * *

Since antiquity, one of the key principles of philosophy has been the idea of freedom. Philosophers from many different schools have looked into the idea of freedom and how to get it. One school of philosophy that has particularly highlighted the idea of freedom is Stoicism. In the third century BC, Zeno of Citium founded the ancient Greek philosophy known as stoicism. Stoics believe that freedom is not only a bodily state but also a state of mind that may be acquired through reason and self-control. In this essay, we shall examine the Stoic conception of freedom and its attainment.

According to the Stoics, freedom is not only the absence of physical restrictions but also the absence of mental ones. To gain full freedom, one must be free from emotional and mental restrictions that limit our ability to reason and act sensibly. Stoics say that freedom

Becoming Stoic

can be reached by practicing virtue, which means living in line with reason and the natural order of things. Stoics believe that if you live a moral life, you can find inner peace and be free from both internal and external limits.

Stoics put a lot of weight on the fact that you need self-control and logic to be free. They believe that in order to prevent one's emotions and desires from controlling them, one should be able to do so. This means that one should not be pushed or hindered by their emotions or desires, but rather should be able to make sensible decisions that are in line with their values and aims. Stoics believe that by exercising self-control and logic, one can achieve true freedom and live a satisfying life.

Stoics also think that freedom can be reached by accepting the natural order of things. According to Stoic philosophy, everything that happens is a result of the natural order of things, and as such, one should not reject or attempt to change it. Stoics believe that if you accept the way things are meant to be, you can find inner peace and be free from outside restrictions. This means that one should not be limited by external factors such as wealth, social status, or material possessions, but rather should focus on developing their inner self.

Stoics stress how important it is to live in the present moment if you want to be free. They hold that one should live in the present and make the most of it rather than dwell on the past or worry about the future. Stoics believe that by living in the present moment, one can reach a sense of inner serenity and freedom from external constraints.

Stoics also believe that living a simple, cheap life can lead to freedom. They believe that one should not be attached to material possessions or wealth, but rather, should focus on living a simple and virtuous life. Stoics believe that by living a simple and modest life, one can gain freedom from external limitations such as the need for wealth or social status.

In conclusion, the Stoics think that virtue, self-control, and reason are the keys to real freedom. They think that by accepting the natural order of things and living in the present moment, one can achieve

True Freedom

inner peace and freedom from external constraints. Stoics also highlight the value of living a modest and frugal life and not being attached to material possessions or fortune. With the practice of Stoic philosophy, one can gain a sense of inner freedom that allows them to live a full and ethical life.

Opinions of Others

"I will not care about the opinions of others."

* * *

One of the key principles of Stoicism is the statement, "I will not care about the opinions of others." Stoicism's primary theme is that people can find peace and happiness by concentrating on the things they can control and accepting the things they cannot, including other people's opinions.

People's opinions are seen as external, uncontrollable things from a stoic perspective. There will always be those who disapprove of, judge, or disagree with one's actions. The Stoic approach to dealing with this fact is to concentrate on one's own ideas, deeds, and emotions because those are things that one can control. According to stoics, cultivating an outlook that is unaffected by other people's perspectives will help people nurture an inner sense of serenity and contentment.

This does not imply that Stoics are unconcerned with other people's emotions or viewpoints. Instead, they understand that they

Becoming Stoic

have no influence over what other people think or feel and that basing one's happiness or sense of value on other people is counter-productive. The actions, ideas, and feelings that one chooses to experience are all things that one has control over, according to the Stoics.

To develop a sense of detachment from external results is one of the essential Stoic strategies for obtaining this mindset. This means that you have to accept that you can't control the results and that what matters most is how you go about achieving your goals. Stoics stress how important it is to focus on the process of living a good life instead of getting stuck on certain goals or results.

Practically speaking, this means that stoics make an effort to live up to their own ideals and principles, regardless of pressure or opinions from others. They understand that they have the ability to control their behavior and can decide how to react to outside situations. Stoics can find inner peace and happiness that don't depend on what's going on around them by focusing on their own actions and the process of living a good life.

The value of self-analysis and reflection is another theme of stoicism. People can better grasp their own values and priorities by taking a close look at their own thoughts and feelings. People who are more self-aware are better able to make thoughtful decisions and uphold their own morals, rather than succumbing to pressure or ideas from others.

Stoics also agree that people need to learn to care about and understand other people. They acknowledge that other people have their own troubles and challenges, even though they do not base their sense of happiness or self-worth on those of others. By developing a sense of empathy and compassion, people can better understand the points of view of others and form stronger bonds.

In conclusion, "I will not care about the opinions of others," is one of the most important ideas in stoicism. People's opinions are seen as external, uncontrollable things from a stoic perspective. Stoics advocate concentrating on one's own ideas, deeds, and emotions rather than on factors outside of one's control. Individuals can build a sense

Opinions of Others

of inner peace and contentment that is unaffected by external circumstances by creating a sense of detachment from external results, growing self-awareness and introspection, and developing empathy and compassion for others. Although putting the Stoic tenets into practice can be difficult, they provide a strong framework for leading a happy and purposeful life.

Chapter 4
UNBIASED THOUGHT

Master of Your Mind

"I am the master of my own mind."

* * *

The idea that "I am the master of my own mind" is a fundamental principle of Stoicism, a philosophy that has been around for over two millennia. At its core, Stoicism is about personal responsibility, self-control, and living a life of virtue. This philosophy teaches that we have the power to control our thoughts and emotions, and that by doing so, we can live a life of tranquility, inner peace, and happiness.

According to the Stoics, the human mind is the most powerful force in the universe. They believed that we have the ability to control our thoughts and that our thoughts, in turn, shape our emotions and actions. According to this philosophy, our thoughts and emotions are within our control, and we can choose to respond to any situation in a rational and virtuous way.

The Stoics thought that the best way to control our own minds was to be self-aware and discipline ourselves. They taught that we should pay attention to our thoughts and feelings and try to develop a

Becoming Stoic

calm, logical mind. By practicing self-discipline, we can learn to respond to situations calmly and logically instead of letting our emotions take over.

One of the ways that the Stoics practiced self-discipline was through the use of negative visualization. This technique involves imagining the worst-case scenario in any situation and then mentally preparing oneself for that outcome. By doing so, one can develop the resilience and inner strength to face any situation with equanimity, no matter how difficult or challenging it may be.

Another key aspect of Stoicism is the idea of living in accordance with nature. The Stoics believed that everything in the universe is linked and that we should strive to live in harmony with nature. This means living a simple and frugal lifestyle and not being attached to material possessions or worldly desires. By living in accordance with nature, we can develop a sense of inner peace and tranquility.

The Stoics also thought that it was important to develop good traits like wisdom, courage, fairness, and self-control. These virtues were seen as the key to living a life of excellence and fulfilling one's potential as a human being. By practicing these virtues, we can build the character and inner strength to face any challenge with courage and grace.

In conclusion, the idea that "I am the master of my own mind" is a central principle of Stoicism This philosophy teaches that we have the power to control our thoughts and emotions, and that by doing so, we can live a life of tranquility, inner peace, and happiness. Through self-awareness, self-discipline, and the cultivation of virtues, we can develop the resilience and inner strength to face any situation with equanimity and grace. In a world that is often chaotic and unpredictable, the teachings of Stoicism offer a timeless and profound wisdom that can help us navigate the challenges of life with wisdom and courage.

On Making Hasty Decisions

"I will not make hasty decisions and judgements."

* * *

The Stoic philosophy places a strong emphasis on the value of reason and self-control in leading a happy life. The Stoics think that making quick decisions and judgments goes against this way of thinking because they are often based on feelings instead of thinking. In this essay, we'll look at why the Stoics thought this way and how their philosophy can affect how people make decisions.

The first argument given by the Stoics for their view is the fact that hasty decisions and judgments are frequently based on feelings rather than logic. Stoics understand the importance of emotions because they are a natural part of being human. They know, though, that feelings can make it hard to think straight and make people act in ways that aren't in their best interests. Because of this, Stoics encourage moderation and logical thinking as a way to keep emotions from clouding judgment.

Becoming Stoic

The practice of mindfulness is one method the Stoics use to promote rational thought. Being mindful means paying attention to one's thoughts, emotions, and physiological reactions without passing judgment. People can better understand their emotions and how they affect their decisions by engaging in mindfulness practices. Those who are aware of this can make more wise decisions that are not only influenced by their emotions.

The Stoics say that you shouldn't make quick decisions or judgments because they could have long-term effects. The Stoics hold that everything in life is interrelated and that there are repercussions for every choice that is made. If a decision is made based on an instinct or emotion that comes up quickly, it could cause problems in the future. The Stoics stress that people should think about how their choices might affect them in the long run before making them.

The Stoic philosophy also promotes personal accountability for one's decisions. This means accepting the results of one's actions and acting to change any unfavorable effects. Individuals can learn from their mistakes and make better decisions in the future by accepting responsibility for their decisions.

The Stoics know that making hasty decisions and judgments can lead to trouble and hurt other people. Making a choice without taking into account how it may affect others might have unfavorable effects and damage relationships. The Stoics also promote giving thought to other people's needs and emotions when making decisions.

Living in harmony with nature is another important principle of the Stoic philosophy. This means recognizing that everything in life is temporary and that change is a normal aspect of the experience of being alive. People can make decisions that are in keeping with their goals and principles rather than being motivated by a desire to control or fight change by accepting this truth.

In the end, the Stoic philosophy tells us not to make snap decisions or judgments because they are often based on feelings instead of logic. The Stoics advise people to live in harmony with nature, culti-

On Making Hasty Decisions

vate mindfulness, think about the long-term effects of their actions, accept responsibility for them, and think about the needs and feelings of others. People can make better judgments that result in a more fulfilling life by adhering to these principles.

Focusing on Self-Improvement

"I will focus on self-improvement."

* * *

Throughout history, the idea of self-improvement has been central to philosophical and psychological research. From antiquity to the present, scholars have extensively studied and discussed the idea of self-improvement. In this lesson, I'll examine the idea of self-improvement from the standpoint of stoicism, one of history's most important philosophical movements.

Stoicism teaches that one of the best ways to live a happy and meaningful life is to learn to be self-disciplined and in charge of yourself. The Stoics held that people can achieve happiness and inner peace by placing more value on their own character and virtue than on things like wealth, power, or celebrity. In this sense, self-improvement was viewed as the ultimate objective of human existence.

The Stoics say that the best way to get better is to develop virtues like wisdom, courage, self-control, fairness, and kindness. These virtues were regarded as necessary for living well and finding inner peace. The Stoics held that these characteristics could be developed through self-reflection and regular practice because they were not natural. In other words, self-improvement was a continuous process of progress and self-discovery rather than a singular occurrence.

The idea of "the dichotomy of control" is one of the main tenets of Stoicism. The concept behind this belief is that people have control over their own ideas and behaviors, but not over other situations or events. The Stoics believed that people should concentrate on the things they can control and accept the things they cannot. This means that self-improvement shouldn't try to change things like other people's opinions or the way things go. Instead, it should focus on developing internal qualities like virtue.

The idea of "the present moment" is another key Stoic concept. The Stoics held that people should not worry about the past or the future but rather concentrate on the present. This means that rather than concentrating on the past or worrying about the future, self-improvement should concentrate on the now. People can practice mindfulness and find inner peace and contentment by paying attention to the present moment.

The Stoics also stressed the importance of self-reflection and self-awareness for personal growth. Stoics thought that people should always look at their own thoughts, beliefs, and actions to see where they could improve. This means that if you want to grow as a person, you should always be looking inward and judging yourself.

A Stoic view of self-improvement includes the development of inner fortitude and tenacity. The Stoics held that people should welcome obstacles and hardships as chances for personal improvement. This implies that self-improvement should be viewed as a difficult and demanding process rather than as something simple or comfortable. Individuals can build resilience and inner strength, which are necessary for leading a successful and meaningful life, by accepting obstacles and challenges.

From a Stoic point of view, the best way to improve yourself is to develop a strong sense of purpose and meaning in life. The Stoics

Focusing on Self-Improvement

believed that people should try to live by their own ideals and principles rather than letting things like their social standing or financial status influence them. This means that a serious look at one's own ideas and values, as well as the desire to live by them, are important parts of self-improvement.

From a Stoic point of view, self-improvement means getting better at things like wisdom, courage, self-control, justice, and compassion, as well as building resilience and inner strength. It also means constantly thinking about and examining oneself, paying attention to the present, and having a strong sense of meaning and purpose.

A Mental Fortress

"I won't let someone's words or actions hurt my mind."

***

Stoicism is based on the idea that you should have no feelings and stay calm when things are hard. It shows how important it is to control one's emotions and keep outside influences from changing one's mind.

The best way to describe the stoic way of thinking is with the phrase, "I won't let someone's words or actions hurt my mind." Stoicism says that mental injury is a kind of self-harm that comes from a person's own thoughts and feelings. The Stoics hold that neither what happens to a person nor what other people do can harm them; only their own thoughts can.

The stoic view stresses how important it is to take responsibility for one's own thoughts and actions. It implies that we have the freedom to decide how to react, regardless of what others may say or

Becoming Stoic

do. It serves as a potent reminder that we are in charge of our own lives and can decide how to respond to the events taking place all around us.

The three main tenets of the stoic approach to mental injury are as follows: Self-awareness is the first principle. The Stoics hold that we need to be conscious of our own ideas and feelings and the effects they have on us. We must also be conscious of our own vulnerabilities and weak points. We can realize when we are at risk of mental injury and take action to stop it thanks to this self-awareness.

Self-control is the second principle. When we become conscious of our thoughts and feelings, we must practice self-control to keep them from hurting us. So that we can stay composed and concentrated in the face of difficulty, we must learn to control our thoughts and emotions.

Resilience is the third guiding principle. The Stoics hold that in order to overcome the obstacles life throws our way, we must develop resilience. We must learn how to overcome challenges and recover from setbacks. A strong sense of purpose, a clear set of values, and a thorough grasp of our own strengths and shortcomings are the foundations of resilience.

The Stoics also say that our own judgments and expectations often hurt our mental health. Because we have distorted perceptions of how other people should behave, we might feel hurt or offended by what they say or do. We can also be hard on ourselves if we have our own ideas about how we should react.

Stoics say that having irrational expectations and making irrational judgments can hurt your mind and should be avoided. Accepting things as they are, we should concentrate on what we can manage. In order to avoid being too impacted by outside events, we should also develop a sense of detachment from them.

Lastly, the stoic way to keep your mind from getting hurt is a powerful reminder of how important it is to take responsibility for your own thoughts and feelings. Having self-awareness, self-control, and resilience can help us build a strong foundation for a happy life.

A Mental Fortress

In order to avoid self-harm, we might learn to remain composed and emotionless in the face of difficulty. The stoic way of thinking serves as a reminder that we are all capable of choosing how we will react to the events taking place all around us and how we will shape our own future.

Committiment to Being Rational

"I will always be rational."

* * *

Stoicism is a way of thinking that puts a lot of weight on reason as a key trait for living a happy, meaningful life. Stoicism is a practical philosophy that tries to help people become more calm and brave when they face problems in life. The idea that people should always try to be rational in their thought and decision-making processes is one of the core principals of Stoicism. In this lesson, we'll look at what Stoicism says about the importance of reason and how people can develop reason as a virtue.

To understand what reason means in Stoicism, you need to know about the larger world in which this philosophy grew up. Stoicism started in ancient Greece around the third century BC. It was a response to the fast changes in politics and society at the time. The Stoics held that it was possible for people to exercise their own mental and emotional control and that this control was crucial for living a happy life. The Stoic concept of "virtue," which refers to the development of inner courage and moral character through the practice of logical reasoning and decision-making, reflects this idea.

Making logical choices was only one aspect of being rational in the eyes of the Stoics. Instead, it was a more expansive worldview that took into account every facet of a person's existence. The Stoic definition of reason is that being rational means living in harmony with nature, which is seen as an all-powerful force that controls everything. This means that instead of attempting to force their own will on the world around them, individuals must align their thoughts and actions with the natural order of things.

In real life, this means that people should make an effort to be unbiased in their thought and decision-making processes. People shouldn't give in to their impulses and feelings. Instead, they should use logic in every part of their lives. This covers everything, from how they handle challenging circumstances to how they communicate with others on a regular basis.

Self-reflection is a technique that people can use to develop rationality in their lives. This means pausing to consider one's own feelings and ideas in order to spot any instances where irrationality may be edging in. One might need to take a step back and reflect on why they are reacting in this way, for instance, if they catch oneself getting angry or upset about a trivial matter. People might start to recognize any biases or preconceptions that might be impairing their judgment by analyzing their own cognitive processes and working to get rid of them.

Learning to manage one's emotions is a crucial part of developing logic in stoicism. The Stoics felt that emotions were one of the biggest obstacles to logical thought since they could impair judgment and cause impulsive behavior. To get over this, people must learn to recognize when their emotions are taking control and take action to regain control and reason. Deep breathing, mindfulness meditation, or simply taking a minute to step back and clear one's thoughts can all be used to achieve this.

The Stoics thought that, in addition to developing reason within

Committtiment to Being Rational

themselves, people should try to live in harmony with others. This involves being kind, sympathetic, and respectful to other people—even when things are difficult. Individuals can do this to build a sense of community and mutual support that will allow them to face life's problems.

The core idea behind the Stoic philosophy of reason is that people may take charge of their own lives by developing their inner courage and resilience. People can live a logical life instead of being led by their emotions or whims if they always try to be reasonable when they think and make decisions.

Chapter 5
RIGHT ACTION

Being Recognized as a Stoic

> **"I will let my actions and character illustrate my understanding of stoicism."**

* * *

According to the Stoic philosophy, people should live in harmony with nature and nurture virtue and wisdom. It shows how important it is to live a good life by strengthening one's character and using self-control, logic, and courage. Stoics try to get better as people by focusing on what they can control and letting go of what they can't. It is a philosophy that can enable people to live fulfilling lives in spite of hardship.

A person's dedication to living according to the principles of Stoicism is expressed when they say, ""I will let my actions and character illustrate my understanding of Stoicism." A true Stoic is someone who not only understands the philosophy but also lives it out every day. Stoicism's values must be demonstrated through one's actions and character; it is not sufficient to merely read about them or comprehend their ideas on an academic level.

Becoming Stoic

The way we live our lives is more important to a Stoic than what we say or think. The actions and way a person lives their life, not what they claim to believe, define who they are as a person. To put it another way, being a Stoic is not enough; one must also practice what they preach.

The Stoics held that the secret to a happy and satisfying life was to live in harmony with nature. This entailed leading a life of virtue, discernment, and restraint. Also, it meant accepting the things outside of our control and concentrating on those instead. A stoic does not allow external circumstances to affect their happiness or well-being. Instead, they focused their attention on strengthening their inner character and leading moral lives.

To live in harmony with nature, you also have to accept that everything is temporary and will end at some point. The Stoics held that change is the only constant in life and that someday everything we value will be stolen from us. This doesn't imply that we should be pessimistic or indifferent to life; rather, it means that we should treasure each day and recognize the beauty of life while we still have it.

A Stoic thinks that the key to living a good life is to develop virtue and wisdom. A Stoic's character is built on virtue, which also serves as their compass when acting and making judgments. Wisdom, on the other hand, is the ability to see things clearly and understand how things really are. It is the capacity to prioritize what really matters in life and to differentiate between what is under our control and what is not.

Self-control is one of a Stoic's most crucial virtues. A Stoic must develop self-control over their feelings, desires, and urges. They must learn to withstand pressure and refrain from making snap decisions. A Stoic should be in control of their emotions rather than allowing them to control them, which does not imply that they should be emotionless or robotic.

Courage is another quality that a Stoic should possess. A Stoic must develop the courage and fortitude to deal with difficulties and hardship. People need to be prepared to take chances and confront

Being Recognized as a Stoic

their concerns. This does not imply that a Stoic should be careless or foolish, but rather that they should be ready to face difficulties and take appropriate action.

A Stoic must also practice compassion and empathy as their final virtues. They must learn to be courteous and respectful to others and to understand other people's viewpoints. To be clear, this does not imply that a Stoic should be a pushover or let others treat them badly; rather, it indicates that a Stoic should treat others with the same respect and consideration that they would expect for themselves.

In conclusion, when someone vows to live their life in accordance with the Stoic principles, they are saying, ""I will let my actions and character illustrate my understanding of Stoicism," of cultivating a strong mental capability, courage, wisdom, moderation, and self-control. They are dedicated to developing their stoicism and living their philosophy.

Doing the Right Thing

"I will find pleasure in doing the right thing."

* * *

One of the core concepts of Stoicism is that real contentment and happiness can only be achieved by following reason and making an effort to act morally at all times. Stoicism is based on the idea that happiness and pleasure are not the same thing and that chasing pleasure for its own sake is ultimately pointless and can lead to a morally corrupt life.

One of the ultimate goals for the stoic is to take pleasure in doing what is right. This means that the stoic will enjoy doing the right thing, even if it is challenging or uncomfortable, since they know it is the right thing to do. Since most individuals link pleasure with satisfying feelings or sensations, this may seem paradoxical. The stoic perspective, however, holds that any action that is in line with one's moral code can bring about pleasure.

Because they are aware that their own actions are the only thing actually within their control, the stoic takes joy in doing what is right.

Becoming Stoic

Although individuals have no control over what other people do or the situation they are in, they do have control over how they choose to react. The stoic takes charge of their life and enjoys knowing that they are living up to their own standards by making decisions that are consistent with reason and morality.

It is crucial to remember that the Stoic does not always find it simple or enjoyable to act morally. In actuality, it frequently necessitates a great deal of self-control and persistence. The stoic, however, realizes that the task's difficulties are pointless. What counts is that they are acting morally and leading a life of virtue, and that is what matters.

The concept of the control dilemma is another part of stoicism that pertains to enjoying doing the right thing. The stoic understands that some aspects of life are under their control and others are not. They also know that trying to control things they can't change will only make them feel frustrated and hopeless. Instead, the stoic directs their attention and energy toward the things that they can influence, notably their own decisions and responses to the external environment.

The stoic is able to take joy in doing the right thing, even in challenging or unpleasant situations, by concentrating on what they have control over. They are aware that, while they have no control over the results of their actions, they do have control over the intentions that led to those behaviors. They feel content when they follow their moral principles because they know they are doing the right thing, no matter what happens.

In conclusion, a fundamental principle of stoicism is finding joy in doing the right thing. For the stoic, contentment and happiness are only possible through living in line with reason and morals and making an effort to always act morally. The stoic finds joy in even the most difficult or disagreeable jobs by concentrating on what is under their control and acting in accordance with their own moral code. The stoic recognizes that true pleasure comes from leading a moral life and doing what is right, regardless of the result, even though it

Doing the Right Thing

may seem contradictory to find pleasure in doing something that is challenging or painful.

It is important to know that being known as a Stoic because of your actions and character is different from trying to get praise or attention. Stoics believe that true virtue comes from within and doesn't need approval or reward from the outside world. Instead, a Stoic cares more about living a good life for its own sake than about getting praise or rewards from other people.

Put it to Practice

"I will put into practice the lessons I learn from Stoicism."

* * *

To put Stoic ideas into practice, you have to live in a way that is based on logic, self-control, and discipline. It means being aware of our thoughts, feelings, and actions and trying to live according to our values and principles.

Stoicism is based on the principle that we should try to live in harmony with nature. This does not mean going off to live in the bush or becoming a hermit; rather, it means living in accordance with the natural order of things. The Stoics also thought that the laws of reason that govern the universe were a part of nature. To live in harmony with nature, we must join our will with the will of the universe, accept what happens, and stop resisting or trying to control things that are out of our control.

Focusing on what we can control and letting go of what we cannot is one of the key tenets of stoicism. This suggests that we

Becoming Stoic

should concentrate on our own ideas, emotions, and behaviors rather than wasting time and effort on things we cannot change. We should try to be self-sufficient and not depend on things outside of ourselves to make us happy or healthy.

The idea of the dichotomy of control is another crucial Stoic principle. This is the belief that there are certain things we can control, like our ideas, emotions, and behaviors, and some things we can't, like other people's actions or the weather. The Stoics held that we should concentrate on what we can control and not worry about what we cannot.

Stoicism also teaches us the value of living in the here and now. The only time that truly matters is now because the past is gone and the future is unclear. We may fully interact with our lives and fully appreciate the wonder and beauty of the world around us by staying in the here and now.

It takes discipline and work to put the Stoic principles into effect. We must develop a daily practice of self-reflection and self-awareness. Making decisions that are conscious and consistent with our beliefs and ideals requires that we work to be aware of our thoughts, emotions, and behaviors.

Stoicism focuses on how important it is to have inner strength and courage when things get hard. We must learn to accept what occurs and control our emotions. So that we may approach issues with clarity and composure, we must establish a feeling of detachment and objectivity.

The idea of the "view from above" is one of Stoicism's most potent lessons. This is the notion that we ought to see ourselves viewing our lives from a higher vantage point, similar to a bird's-eye view. By doing this, we can acquire perspective and put our issues in a larger context. We can come to the realization that our issues are not as important as we believe they are and that the universe is far bigger than ourselves.

In conclusion, putting Stoic ideas into action requires self-control, effort, and a regular practice of self-reflection and self-aware-

Put it to Practice

ness. It means living in harmony with nature, focusing on what we can control, building inner strength and resilience, and getting a sense of objectivity and distance. By following these rules, we can live in a good way and give ourselves the strength to deal with whatever life throws at us. I will make an effort to live according to these Stoic principles.

Daily Improvement

"I will focus on myself and work daily to improve."

* * *

Stoicism teaches that the path to a prosperous life begins with understanding and improving oneself. This journey starts by focusing on what is within our control—our thoughts, attitudes, and actions—while accepting what we cannot control, such as external events and other people's actions. By directing our energy towards self-improvement, we can build a stronger, more resilient character.

Being self-aware is one of the first steps in this process. Understanding our habits, mental patterns, abilities, and shortcomings is the first step toward bettering ourselves. Being self-aware enables us to see our areas for improvement and constructive transformation. Recognizing a pattern, such as your frequent rage reaction in stressful situations, is the first step to improving the way you control your reactions. We can start making deliberate decisions that are consistent with our beliefs and objectives.

Setting clear and attainable goals for progress comes next, when

Becoming Stoic

we have a firm grasp of who we are. These objectives ought to be in line with our beliefs and centered on fostering characteristics like discernment, bravery, justice, and temperance. If wisdom is important to you, for example, you could make it a goal to read and learn new things on a regular basis. If bravery is important to you, you may push yourself to overcome your worries and do new things. Establishing specific objectives gives our attempts at self-improvement focus and inspiration.

Personal improvement requires consistency. Daily self-improvement calls for commitment and discipline. It entails putting in little but steady effort to change our attitudes, behaviors, and routines. For instance, you may start by setting aside a short period of time each day for mindful breathing exercises or meditation if you want to make mindfulness a habit. These modest daily routines have the potential to significantly enhance your mental and emotional health over time.

Accepting obstacles and disappointments as opportunities for personal development is another critical component of self-improvement. Adversity is an unavoidable aspect of life, according to stoicism, but how we handle hardships shapes who we are as people. Instead of viewing setbacks as failures, we can view them as important lessons that make us stronger and wiser. For example, rather than giving up when something goes wrong at work, such as a project not working out as expected, consider the lessons you learned from it and how you may use them in the future. This viewpoint encourages us to grow resilient and have a positive outlook on obstacles.

Self-reflection exercises are an effective tool for personal development. We can better understand our behaviors and make necessary adjustments by routinely reflecting on our choices, experiences, and actions. You could spend time at the end of each day reflecting on how you handled different situations, what you did well, and what you could improve. This technique helps to highlight constructive conduct and identify areas for improvement.

The development of inner virtues is a crucial component of stoic self-improvement. To be wise, one must make deliberate and well-

Daily Improvement

informed choices. Being courageous means having the fortitude to face obstacles and fears. Justice entails treating people fairly and with dignity. Being temperate entails using restraint and moderation. By focusing on these characteristics, we can direct our behaviors and decisions toward a more moral and satisfying existence.

Using wisdom, for example, might entail doing research and gathering information before making critical decisions. Taking on new challenges and moving outside of your comfort zone can be necessary for developing courage. Maintaining justice may entail showing compassion and decency to others, especially in trying circumstances.

Focusing on Now

"I will focus on what is happening now, even if it is something I don't want to do."

* * *

Stoicism stresses how important it is to live in harmony with nature, find inner peace, and pay attention to the present moment. Stoicism is based on the idea that we can choose how to react to things outside of ourselves, regardless of whether we can control them or not.

To focus on what is happening now, even if it is something we don't want to do, is to represent this Stoic ideal. It means recognizing and accepting the facts of the present moment, even if they are hard or uncomfortable. This doesn't mean that we should give up on our goals or dreams. Instead, it means that we should focus on what we can control, which is our own actions and attitudes.

From a Stoic point of view, the best way to stay in the present is to become aware of how separate you are from outside events. This doesn't mean we should stop caring about the world around us or be

Becoming Stoic

indifferent to it. Instead, it means we should realize that our happiness and well-being don't depend on what's going on outside of us but on how we feel inside. By developing a sense of inner peace and calm, we can learn to face even the most difficult situations with clarity and calmness.

Stoics use negative imagery as one way to develop this sense of being separate from things. This means imagining the worst-case scenario in each situation and getting our minds ready to handle it. By tackling our worries and anxieties in this way, we can learn to appreciate the present moment and the benefits that we have in our lives rather than taking them for granted.

Stoicism is also based on the idea that people should live in harmony with nature. This does not mean just accepting things as they are, but rather realizing that we are part of a bigger system that acts according to its own laws and rhythms. By matching our behaviors and attitudes with these natural principles, we can live in harmony with the world around us and find a sense of purpose and meaning in our lives.

It enables us to let go of our attachment to the past and our concerns about the future in order to focus on what is happening now, even if it is something we don't want to do. Instead, we must learn to accept the present as it is, with all of its flaws and difficulties. On the other hand, it means that we should approach each moment with openness and curiosity and be ready to learn from our experiences and grow from them. This does not imply that we should become complacent or inactive.

In conclusion, adopting the core ideas of Stoic philosophy means paying attention to what is happening right now, even if it is something we don't want to do. This means developing a sense of separation from outside events, seeing the truth of the present moment, and making sure our actions and attitudes are in line with the natural laws that apply to everyone. By living this way, we can find peace and calm within ourselves and be able to respond calmly and logically to

Focusing on Now

even the most difficult situations. At its core, the Stoic ideal is a way of living that may give our lives meaning and purpose while guiding us through the difficulties and uncertainties of the human experience.

Chapter 6
PROBLEM SOLVING

Seeing It For What It Is

"I will see humanity from a high perspective and make notice of the petty nature of political matters."

* * *

By managing their emotions and concentrating on the things they can control, people can live moral lives by following the teachings of the Stoic philosophy. Stoicism says that it's important to keep a "view from above," which means that people should try to see things from a higher point of view. They can learn more about the universe and their place in it by doing this.

Stoicism says that people shouldn't care too much about politics because political issues are usually small. Instead, they ought to concentrate on the things they can influence, including their own deeds and attitudes. This does not imply that people should not be concerned with social justice issues or politics. Instead, it says that people should deal with these problems calmly and logically, without letting their feelings or ideas get in the way.

Focusing on the bigger picture can help politicians develop a

Becoming Stoic

"view from above." Elections and the passage of legislation, among other short-term issues, frequently overshadow politics. These things are significant, yet they are also temporary. People should concentrate on the long-term objectives and principles they hold dear rather than getting sucked into the daily drama of politics. This involves taking a step back and examining the bigger picture of the political environment.

Empathy and compassion exercises are another technique to develop a "view from above." Faced with political unrest and corruption, it is easy to grow jaded and cynical. Yet, Stoicism advises people to approach politics with an open mind and a readiness to consider other people's viewpoints. They will be better able to comprehend the problems at hand and come up with solutions that are advantageous to everyone if they do this.

Finally, it's critical to keep in mind that politics is not the only way to change the world. Politics can be quite effective, but there are lots of other ways to bring about change. For instance, people can donate their time and money to charitable organizations or concentrate on their own development and progress. People can make a significant difference in the world by developing their own virtue and making an effort to have a beneficial impact on others around them.

Finally, the Stoic approach to politics emphasizes a "view from above" and a focus on the factors that people may influence. People can make it through the complicated world of politics if they stay calm and logical, show empathy and compassion, and focus on their long-term goals and values. Although political activity can be helpful, it's vital to keep in mind that there are a variety of other ways to change the world for the better. No matter what the political situation is, the Stoic view of politics tells people to live moral lives and help the people around them.

Adjusting Course

"I will commit to a course of action and be watchful to adjust if needed."

* * *

Stoicism is a branch of philosophy that says the best way to live a good life is to use reason, be moderate, and accept your fate. Stoicism is all about taking responsibility for your own actions and recognizing that you can't change things outside of yourself.

Many of the central principles of Stoicism are expressed in the statement, "I will commit to a course of action and be watchful to adjust if needed." This sentence is mostly about doing something and taking responsibility for what happens as a result. It's about realizing that we have control over our lives and that we need to take an active role in making decisions about our future.

The statement also says that we need to be able to change and stay alert at the same time. It's not enough to choose a course of action and then stick to it without asking how things are going. We must be

Becoming Stoic

ready to change our plan as needed and be open to criticism and new information.

The idea that we should concentrate on what is under our control and let go of what is out of our control is one of the fundamental pillars of stoicism. This means that we should focus on the things we can control, like our own thoughts, actions, and feelings. At the same time, we have to accept that we can't change many things in life, such as natural disasters, how people act, and even our own deaths.

We can use this control principle in our everyday lives by making a plan and keeping an eye out for ways to change it if we need to. We can set objectives, actively work towards them, and be aware that as things change, we might need to modify our strategy.

Stoicism also emphasizes the importance of living in harmony with nature. This entails being mindful of our modest place in the universe and living in peace with the natural environment. We may align our actions with the natural progression of events and prevent the tension and worry that result from attempting to manage things that are out of our control by committing to a course of action and remaining vigilant to make changes as necessary.

This is obviously easier said than done. In the face of hardship, it can be challenging to keep perspective and keep our attention on what is within our power. Yet, stoicism may teach us the tenacity and inner fortitude we require to meet life's problems with composure and grace.

We can develop this resilience in part by engaging in mindfulness exercises. The discipline of mindfulness involves being in the moment without passing judgment. We can let go of concerns about the past and the future by concentrating on the present moment in order to feel peaceful and clear.

The practice of appreciation is another way we may build resilience. The act of noticing and appreciating the positive aspects of our existence is known as gratitude. We can turn our attention away from our difficulties and onto the things that make us happy and fulfilled by practicing appreciation.

Adjusting Course

In the end, taking responsibility for our lives and realizing that we can make our own decisions means committing to a plan of action and keeping an eye out for changes that may be needed. It's about building the strength we need to handle life's challenges with composure and grace. This means being aware of our thoughts and actions and coordinating our actions with how things are going. We can live a life of meaning, fulfillment, and purpose by adhering to these values, even in the face of adversity.

Mental Resilience

"I will have a mentally resilient and flexible defense in life."

***

The Stoics believed that our thoughts and beliefs shape our emotions and actions and that we have the power to choose our thoughts and responses to external events. This ability to control our thoughts and emotions is the foundation of mental resilience and flexibility.

To cultivate mental resilience, Stoics advise us to develop a mindset that accepts and even welcomes adversity. This does not mean that we should seek out difficult situations, but rather that we should approach them with a sense of detachment and objectivity. By accepting that life is inherently unpredictable and that adversity is inevitable, we can prepare ourselves mentally to deal with challenges when they arise.

One way to cultivate mental resilience is through the practice of negative visualization. This involves imagining worst-case scenarios and reflecting on how we would cope with them. By mentally

Becoming Stoic

preparing ourselves for difficult situations, we can reduce the impact of negative events and develop a sense of inner strength and resilience.

Another key aspect of mental resilience is the ability to maintain perspective and avoid getting caught up in our own emotions. This requires a willingness to step back and view situations objectively, rather than being consumed by our own feelings and reactions. By recognizing that our emotions are ultimately under our control, we can develop a sense of calm and inner peace even in the face of difficult circumstances.

Flexibility, on the other hand, is the ability to adapt to changing circumstances and adjust our thoughts and behaviors accordingly. This requires a willingness to be open-minded and receptive to new information, even if it challenges our existing beliefs or assumptions.

Stoics encourage us to cultivate a mindset of curiosity and continuous learning, which can help us remain flexible and adaptable in the face of change. By seeking out new experiences and perspectives, we can expand our understanding of the world and develop a more nuanced and complex view of reality.

Another key aspect of flexibility is the ability to recognize and accept our own limitations. This requires a willingness to be humble and to acknowledge that we do not have all the answers. By recognizing that there is always more to learn and that we can benefit from the insights and expertise of others, we can remain open-minded and receptive to new ideas and perspectives.

In addition to these individual practices, the Stoic philosophy emphasizes the importance of cultivating strong social connections and relationships. By building a network of supportive friends and family, we can find comfort and strength in times of adversity and benefit from the wisdom and experience of those around us.

At the same time, Stoics recognize that our relationships with others are ultimately beyond our control and that we must be prepared to accept loss and change. This requires a willingness to let

Mental Resilience

go of attachments and to focus on what we can control rather than being consumed by our own desires and expectations.

In conclusion, the Stoic philosophy offers a powerful framework for developing mental resilience and flexibility in life. By cultivating a mindset of acceptance, objectivity, and adaptability, we can prepare ourselves to face life's challenges with strength and grace. Through practices such as negative visualization, curiosity, and building strong social connections, we can develop the inner resources and support systems necessary to weather the storms of life. While the road to mental resilience and flexibility may not be easy, it is ultimately a path that leads to greater peace, happiness, and fulfillment in life.

Forgiving Yourself

"I will forgive myself when I make mistakes."

* * *

The concept of self-forgiveness is central to leading a fulfilling life. To forgive oneself is to acknowledge that we are humans and therefore prone to making mistakes. It is an act of recognizing our fallibility and accepting our shortcomings with a compassionate and non-judgmental attitude.

Stoicism teaches us that we should not be too harsh on ourselves when we make mistakes, as it is part of the natural human experience. In fact, the Stoics believed that making mistakes was essential for personal growth and development. They argued that it is through our mistakes that we learn valuable lessons that help us become better individuals.

However, this does not mean that we should be complacent about our mistakes. Instead, we should take responsibility for our actions and strive to correct them in the best way possible. This is where self-forgiveness comes in. By forgiving ourselves, we can let go of the past and focus on the present moment, which is where true progress can be made.

Self-forgiveness requires us to cultivate a sense of self-compassion. It involves treating ourselves with the same kindness and understanding that we would offer to a close friend who is going through a difficult time. This means acknowledging our mistakes and taking steps to rectify them, while at the same time refraining from self-criticism and negative self-talk.

In the Stoic tradition, self-forgiveness is seen as a fundamental aspect of self-improvement. It is through forgiving ourselves that we can overcome our mistakes and move forward with greater clarity and purpose. By recognizing that we are not perfect and accepting our imperfections, we can cultivate a sense of humility and gratitude, which are essential virtues for living a fulfilling life.

Moreover, self-forgiveness is closely linked to the Stoic concept of rationality. The Stoics believed that rationality was the key to living a good life, as it allowed us to see things clearly and make wise decisions. Rationality involves recognizing our emotions and thoughts and then using reason to evaluate them and determine the best course of action.

Negative emotions like guilt, shame, and regret frequently accompany us when we make a mistake. These emotions can cloud our judgment and prevent us from making rational decisions. However, by practicing self-forgiveness, we can overcome these emotions and approach our mistakes with a rational and clear-minded attitude.

Self-forgiveness also plays a crucial role in our relationships with others. When we forgive ourselves, we are more likely to forgive others for their mistakes as well. This allows us to cultivate greater empathy and compassion towards others, which in turn strengthens our social bonds and enhances our sense of community.

In conclusion, from a Stoic perspective, self-forgiveness is an essential aspect of living a fulfilling life. It requires us to acknowledge our mistakes, take responsibility for our actions, and cultivate a sense

Forgiving Yourself

of self-compassion. By forgiving ourselves, we can let go of the past and focus on the present moment, which is where true progress can be made. It allows us to approach our mistakes with a rational and clear-minded attitude and cultivate greater empathy and compassion towards others. Ultimately, self-forgiveness is a path towards personal growth and self-improvement, which are central values in the Stoic tradition.

Proper Prior Planning

"I will develop a plan for what might go wrong."

* * *

The Stoics believed in the importance of preparation and being proactive in life rather than simply reacting to situations as they arise. Developing a plan for what might go wrong is an essential part of this philosophy.

To begin with, the Stoics emphasized the importance of being mindful of the potential risks and challenges that we may face in life. This involves taking a realistic and objective view of our circumstances and identifying any possible sources of adversity. By doing so, we can avoid being caught off guard and respond more effectively to challenges when they do arise.

However, the Stoics also recognized that it was not enough to simply be aware of potential problems. We must also take active steps to prepare for them. This means developing a plan of action that will help us mitigate the risks and overcome any obstacles that we may encounter.

Becoming Stoic

One of the key principles of Stoicism is that we should focus on what is within our control and let go of what is beyond our control. When it comes to developing a plan for what might go wrong, this means focusing on the things that we can do to prepare for potential challenges rather than worrying about things that are beyond our control.

For example, if we are concerned about the possibility of losing our job, we can take steps to improve our job skills, build our professional network, and save money in case of a financial emergency. These are all things that are within our control and that can help us be better prepared for the future.

At the same time, the Stoics also recognized that there are some things that are beyond our control. For example, we cannot control the actions of others, the weather, or global economic conditions. Rather than wasting our energy worrying about these things, the Stoics advised focusing on our own attitudes and behaviors and developing the resilience and inner strength needed to face whatever challenges may come our way.

In developing a plan for what might go wrong, the Stoics also emphasized the importance of flexibility and adaptability. While it is important to have a plan in place, we must also be willing to adjust and adapt our plans as circumstances change. This means being open to new information, reassessing our priorities, and being willing to try different approaches if our initial plan proves to be ineffective.

Finally, the Stoics believed that developing a plan for what might go wrong was not just about protecting ourselves from harm but also about cultivating a sense of inner peace and tranquility. By taking proactive steps to prepare for potential challenges, we can reduce our anxiety and uncertainty and feel more in control of our lives. This, in turn, can lead to greater emotional resilience, a sense of purpose and meaning, and a deeper appreciation for the present moment.

In conclusion, developing a plan for what might go wrong is an essential part of Stoic philosophy. By being mindful of potential risks and challenges, focusing on what is within our control, being flexible

Proper Prior Planning

and adaptable, and cultivating a sense of inner peace and tranquility, we can prepare ourselves to face whatever challenges life may bring. While we cannot always control what happens to us, we can control how we respond to it, and the Stoics believed that developing a proactive and resilient mindset is the key to living a fulfilling and meaningful life.

Chapter 7
DUTY

Making A Difficult Decision

"I will make the right decision, even if it is difficult."

* * *

Making the right decision can be a difficult task, but for the Stoics, it is crucial to act in accordance with reason and virtue. Stoicism is a philosophy that teaches individuals to live in harmony with nature and to accept what is outside of their control. It emphasizes the importance of living a virtuous life, which is achieved through the use of reason, self-control, and a sense of duty to others. Therefore, for a Stoic, making the right decision is not only about doing what is morally right but also about acting in accordance with the natural order of things.

The first step towards making the right decision, according to Stoicism, is to understand what is within our control and what is not. This idea is embodied in the famous Stoic dichotomy of control, which distinguishes between things that are up to us (our thoughts, attitudes, and actions) and things that are not (external events and circumstances). A Stoic recognizes that external events are beyond

Becoming Stoic

their control and, therefore, they should focus on what is within their power. This means that they should not be attached to external outcomes but instead focus on doing the right thing.

When faced with a difficult decision, a Stoic would approach it with reason and rationality. They would carefully consider the facts and analyze the situation from all angles. They would then make a decision based on what is morally right, rather than what is easy or convenient. For a Stoic, making the right decision is not about personal gain or avoiding discomfort but rather about acting in accordance with their moral principles.

Moreover, a Stoic understands that making the right decision often requires them to face their fears and overcome their emotions. They recognize that emotions such as fear, anger, and anxiety can cloud their judgment and lead them astray. Therefore, they practice self-control and discipline to overcome their emotions and act in accordance with reason. This requires a great deal of inner strength and resilience, but for a Stoic, it is a necessary part of living a virtuous life.

In addition, a Stoic recognizes that making the right decision often requires them to act in the interest of others rather than their own self-interest. They understand that they are part of a larger community and have a duty to contribute to the greater good. Therefore, they consider the impact of their decisions on others and act in a way that benefits society as a whole. This is a manifestation of the Stoic concept of cosmopolitanism, which emphasizes the idea that all human beings are members of the same community and should act accordingly.

Finally, a Stoic accepts the consequences of their decisions, whether they are positive or negative. They understand that they cannot control external outcomes but can only control their own actions. Therefore, they do not dwell on the past or worry about the future but instead focus on the present moment and do what is right in the here and now. This is a manifestation of the Stoic concept of

Making A Difficult Decision

living in accordance with nature, which emphasizes the importance of accepting the present moment as it is.

In conclusion, for a Stoic, making the right decision, even if it is difficult, is a necessary part of living a virtuous life. It requires them to act in accordance with reason and virtue, to overcome their emotions and fears, and to consider the impact of their decisions on others. It also requires them to accept the consequences of their decisions and live in harmony with nature. Making the right decision is not always easy, but for a Stoic, it is a necessary part of living a good life.

Receiving the Will of the Universe

"I will view myself as fortunate to receive the will of the universe."

* * *

The Stoics believed in the idea of fate and the universe having a predetermined plan. They taught that the universe is rational and that everything that happens, including our own actions, is a part of this plan. This belief is rooted in the Stoic concept of *logos*, which refers to the universal reason or intelligence that governs the universe.

As a Stoic, when you say, "I will view myself as fortunate to receive the will of the universe," you are acknowledging the power of fate and the importance of accepting whatever comes your way. This statement reflects the Stoic idea of embracing the present moment and living in accordance with nature. It implies that you are willing to let go of your own desires and expectations and surrender to the will of the universe.

The Stoics believed that all things happen for a reason and that

Becoming Stoic

there is a purpose to everything. They believed that we should not resist the will of the universe but instead accept it with gratitude and learn from it. This acceptance allows us to live in harmony with nature and find peace within ourselves.

By viewing oneself as fortunate to receive the will of the universe, one is accepting responsibility for their own actions and their consequences. The Stoics believed in the concept of self-control and the importance of being virtuous. They taught that we should strive to live a life of moral excellence and act in accordance with reason and nature.

The Stoics believed that it is not what happens to us that matters, but how we react to it. By viewing oneself as fortunate to receive the will of the universe, one is taking a positive approach to whatever situation they may find themselves in. This positive approach can help us overcome obstacles and find strength in difficult times.

In addition to accepting the will of the universe, the Stoics also believed in the importance of living in the present moment. They believed that dwelling on the past or worrying about the future was a waste of time and energy. By focusing on the present moment and accepting whatever comes our way, we can find peace and contentment within ourselves.

The Stoics believed in the idea of living a simple and modest life. They taught that material possessions and wealth are not the keys to happiness and that true happiness comes from within. By viewing oneself as fortunate to receive the will of the universe, one is acknowledging that material possessions and wealth are not necessary for happiness.

The Stoics also believed in the idea of universal brotherhood. They taught that all people are connected and that we should treat others with kindness and compassion. By viewing oneself as fortunate to receive the will of the universe, one is acknowledging the importance of treating others with respect and compassion.

In conclusion, viewing oneself as fortunate to receive the will of the universe is a central tenet of Stoic philosophy. It reflects the

Receiving the Will of the Universe

importance of accepting whatever comes our way and living in accordance with nature. By embracing the present moment, accepting responsibility for our actions, and living a virtuous life, we can find peace and contentment within ourselves. The Stoics believed that by following these principles, we could live a life of moral excellence and find true happiness.

Being Honorable, Regardless

"I will do the honorable thing, even if it is difficult or dangerous."

* * *

The idea of doing the honorable thing even in difficult or dangerous situations is a central tenet of Stoicism. Stoics believe that there are certain values that are essential to human flourishing, and honor is one of them. Honor is a quality that we must develop within ourselves through our deeds; it is not something that others can give or take away.

For a Stoic, the honorable thing to do is always the right thing to do. This means that we should act with integrity, even when it is difficult or dangerous. We should not be swayed by fear or desire but instead be guided by reason and virtue. We should act in accordance with our principles, even when doing so requires sacrifice or hardship.

One of the key principles of Stoicism is the idea of living in accordance with nature. This means that we should live in a way that is

Becoming Stoic

consistent with our rational nature as human beings. We should strive to cultivate virtues such as wisdom, courage, justice, and self-control. These virtues are essential to living a good life, and they are also essential to doing the honorable thing.

Wisdom is the foundation of all the other virtues. It is the ability to see things clearly and make wise decisions. When we act with wisdom, we are able to discern what is truly important and act in accordance with our principles. We are able to see beyond the surface of things and understand the deeper meaning of our actions.

Courage is also essential to doing the right thing. It is the ability to face danger or hardship without fear. Courage allows us to act in accordance with our principles, even when doing so requires us to take risks or endure suffering. It is the willingness to stand up for what is right, even when it is unpopular or dangerous.

Justice is another important virtue for a Stoic. It is the ability to act in accordance with fairness and equality. We should treat others with respect and dignity, and we should not allow our own desires or interests to override what is fair and just. Justice requires us to be impartial and to act in the best interests of all, not just ourselves.

Self-control is also essential to doing the right thing. It is the ability to resist temptation and to act in accordance with reason. When we exercise self-control, we are able to resist the pull of our desires and act in accordance with our principles. This allows us to act with integrity, even when it is difficult or dangerous.

In order to do the honorable thing, a Stoic must also be mindful of their own mortality. Death is a natural part of life, and we should not be afraid of it. Instead, we should be mindful of our own mortality and use it as a reminder of the importance of living a good life. We should strive to live in a way that is consistent with our values so that when our time comes, we can face death with dignity and without regret.

In conclusion, the idea of doing the honorable thing even in difficult or dangerous situations is central to Stoic philosophy. It requires us to cultivate virtues such as wisdom, courage, justice, and self-

Being Honorable, Regardless

control and to act in accordance with our principles, even when doing so requires sacrifice or hardship. By living in accordance with nature and being mindful of our own mortality, we can strive to live a good life and do the honorable thing, no matter what the circumstances may be.

Doing What You Love

"**I will do what I love.**"

* * *

Stoicism is a philosophy that emphasizes the importance of reason, virtue, and self-control. It teaches that our emotions and desires should be in harmony with our rational nature and that we should strive to live in accordance with universal moral principles.

According to the Stoics, our passions and desires can be a source of weakness and distraction. When we allow our emotions to control us, we become slaves to our desires and lose the ability to make rational decisions. We may become impulsive, acting on our immediate desires without considering the long-term consequences of our actions. This can lead to a lack of self-control and an erosion of our character.

Instead of pursuing our passions and desires, the Stoics believed that we should focus on cultivating virtues such as wisdom, courage, and justice. By living in accordance with these virtues, we can

Becoming Stoic

achieve a state of inner tranquility and contentment. We can learn to master our emotions and desires rather than letting them control us.

The Stoics recognized that there are things in life that are outside of our control, such as the actions of others, natural disasters, and even our own mortality. However, they believed that we had the power to control our own thoughts and actions. We can choose to live in accordance with virtue, regardless of external circumstances.

In the pursuit of personal fulfillment and happiness, the Stoics believed that we should focus on developing our character and living a virtuous life rather than pursuing our passions and desires. This does not mean that we should not enjoy the things that we love. Rather, we should approach them in a rational and disciplined manner.

For example, if someone loves to play music, they should not abandon all other responsibilities and commitments in order to pursue their passion. Instead, they should approach their music with a sense of discipline and balance. They should set aside time to practice and improve their skills, but they should also prioritize their other obligations, such as work, family, and community.

In this way, the pursuit of one's passions can be integrated into a broader sense of purpose and meaning. Instead of being a source of distraction and weakness, it can be a source of inspiration and motivation.

Furthermore, the Stoics believed that we should be mindful of the things that we love, recognizing that they are ultimately outside of our control. We should not become attached to them or overly invested in them, as this can lead to disappointment and suffering.

Instead, we should approach the things that we love with a sense of detachment and acceptance. We should appreciate them for what they are, but not become overly attached to them or expect them to provide us with lasting happiness.

In conclusion, the phrase "I will do what I love" captures a fundamental human desire for personal fulfillment and happiness. However, from a Stoic perspective, the pursuit of one's passions can

Doing What You Love

be a potentially dangerous pursuit that can lead to a lack of self-control and the degradation of one's character. So, it must always be approached with a watchful eye and regular self-examination.

Instead of pursuing our passions and desires, the Stoics believed that we should focus on cultivating virtues such as wisdom, courage, and justice. By living in accordance with these virtues, we can achieve a state of inner tranquility and contentment. We can learn to master our emotions and desires rather than letting them control us.

This does not mean that we should not enjoy the things that we love. Rather, we should approach them in a rational and disciplined manner, integrating them into a broader sense of purpose and meaning. By doing so, we can find a sense of fulfillment.

Your Duty to Lead

"I will assume a leadership role because it is my duty as a human being to do so."

* * *

Taking on a leadership role can be a daunting task, as it requires one to take responsibility for the well-being of others. However, from a Stoic perspective, assuming a leadership role can be seen as a duty that aligns with the fundamental principles of human nature. This paper will explore the Stoic philosophy and how it relates to the idea of assuming a leadership role.

The central tenet of stoicism is that people should make an effort to lead moral and ethical lives. According to Stoic philosophy, virtue is the only true good, and all other things, such as wealth, power, and fame, are ultimately meaningless. Furthermore, the Stoics believed that individuals have a duty to society and should strive to live in harmony with their fellow human beings.

Assuming a leadership role can be seen as a way to fulfill this duty. As a leader, one has the opportunity to use their reason and

Becoming Stoic

virtue to benefit others. Leadership involves making difficult decisions, taking responsibility for the outcomes of those decisions, and guiding others towards a common goal. Through the act of leadership, one can contribute to the betterment of society and fulfill their duty as a human being.

However, it is important to note that assuming a leadership role does not necessarily mean seeking out positions of power or authority. Instead, it means taking on responsibility for the well-being of others in whatever capacity one is able. This can manifest in a variety of ways, such as by volunteering for community service, mentoring others, or simply being a supportive friend or family member.

In addition to fulfilling one's duty to society, assuming a leadership role can also benefit the individual itself. According to Stoic philosophy, individuals should strive to live in accordance with nature and accept the things that are beyond their control. Through assuming a leadership role, one can develop the virtue of wisdom, which involves understanding the nature of things and making wise decisions based on that understanding.

Furthermore, assuming a leadership role can help individuals develop the virtue of courage. Leadership involves making difficult decisions and taking risks, which can be intimidating. However, by facing these challenges and taking action in spite of fear, individuals can develop the courage necessary to navigate life's challenges.

Assuming a leadership role can also help individuals develop the virtue of justice. As a leader, one has a responsibility to act in the best interest of others and to ensure that everyone is treated fairly. By upholding these principles of justice, individuals can cultivate the virtue of integrity and build trust with those around them.

Of course, assuming a leadership role is not without its challenges. Leaders must be able to navigate difficult situations, make tough decisions, and deal with the consequences of those decisions. They must also be able to balance the needs of others with their own well-being, as neglecting one's own needs can lead to burnout and ultimately harm the very people they are trying to help.

Your Duty to Lead

In order to navigate these challenges, it is important for leaders to cultivate the virtues of humility and self-awareness. Leaders must be willing to acknowledge their own limitations and seek out the advice and support of others when necessary. They must also be willing to reflect on their own actions and behaviors and make changes when necessary.

In conclusion, assuming a leadership role can be seen as a duty that aligns with the fundamental principles of Stoic philosophy. By using reason and virtue to benefit others, individuals can fulfill their duty to society and contribute to the betterment of the world around them. Furthermore, assuming a leadership role can help individuals develop the virtues of wisdom, courage, justice, humility, and self-awareness, which can benefit both the individual and those around them. However, it is important for leaders to approach their role with humility and self-awareness, acknowledging their own limitations and seeking out the advice and support of others when necessary.

Chapter 8
PRAGMATISM

Not Caving to Obstacles

"I will not let obstacles get in the way of what I must do."

* * *

The Stoic philosophy is all about accepting things as they are and focusing on what is within one's control. One of the fundamental principles of Stoicism is the idea of living in accordance with nature, which means being true to one's nature and living a virtuous life. When it comes to overcoming obstacles, Stoicism teaches us to approach them with a mindset of resilience and resourcefulness.

Obstacles are a part of life, and they can come in various forms, such as physical, mental, emotional, or external circumstances. Stoics believe that the only way to deal with obstacles is by facing them head-on and not letting them get in the way of what we must do. This means that we should not let obstacles define us or prevent us from achieving our goals.

The first step towards overcoming obstacles is to recognize that

Becoming Stoic

they exist. We should not deny or ignore them, but rather acknowledge their presence and accept them as part of our reality. The Stoics teach us that the key to dealing with obstacles is to shift our focus from external circumstances to our internal reactions. We can't control what happens to us, but we can control how we react to it.

Stoicism emphasizes the importance of developing a resilient mindset that can withstand any challenges that come our way. This involves cultivating virtues such as courage, wisdom, and self-control, which enable us to face obstacles with a calm and rational mind. Stoics believe that by developing these virtues, we can achieve a state of tranquility and inner peace, even in the midst of adversity.

Another important aspect of Stoic philosophy is the concept of the dichotomy of control. According to this principle, there are two types of things in life; those that are within our control and those that are not. We should focus our energy and attention on the things that are within our control, such as our thoughts, actions, and attitudes. On the other hand, we should not waste our energy on things that are beyond our control, such as other people's opinions or external circumstances.

When it comes to overcoming obstacles, Stoics believe that we should focus on what is within our control and take action accordingly. This means that we should not let external circumstances dictate our actions or determine our destiny. Instead, we should take responsibility for our own lives and make the best of the situation that we find ourselves in.

The Stoics also emphasize the importance of being resourceful in the face of obstacles. This means that we should use our ingenuity and creativity to find new ways of dealing with challenges. We should not be afraid to try new approaches or seek help from others when needed. Stoics believe that by being resourceful, we can overcome any obstacle that comes our way.

In conclusion, Stoicism provides us with a powerful framework for dealing with obstacles. By accepting things as they are, focusing on what is within our control, developing a resilient mindset, and

Not Caving to Obstacles

being resourceful, we can overcome any obstacle that comes our way. The Stoic philosophy teaches us to approach obstacles with courage, wisdom, and self-control and to never let them get in the way of what we must do. In short, Stoicism teaches us to live a virtuous life in accordance with nature, even in the face of adversity.

Doing What is Necessary

"I will be pragmatic and adaptable, always able to do what is needed."

* * *

Stoicism embodies the idea of living in harmony with nature and accepting the world as it is, rather than as we would like it to be. Stoicism teaches us to control what we can and accept what we cannot. By adopting a pragmatic and adaptive attitude, we embrace these values and find ourselves better equipped to tackle obstacles with grace and perseverance.

The core of pragmatism is an emphasis on doable goals and activities that produce positive effects. Rather than relying on rigid ideas or theoretical principles, pragmatism involves making decisions based on what truly works. This entails evaluating the conditions in our day-to-day lives in light of their reality and selecting the best course of action available. Stoic philosophy, which teaches us to accept reality, matches this pragmatic approach.

Conversely, adaptability is the capacity to modify oneself in

Becoming Stoic

response to changing circumstances. The Stoics were well aware of how unpredictable life is by its very nature. Being adaptive makes us pliable and receptive to change, as opposed to being resistant to it. This adaptability enables us to keep our inner serenity despite outside happenings.

Pragmatism and reason are closely associated concepts in Stoic philosophy. Reason helps us come to reasonable and advantageous decisions. A practical response to an issue would be to evaluate it coolly, figure out what we can manage, and act accordingly. We should avoid making poor or ineffective choices due to emotional or wishful thinking.

A pragmatic Stoic approach, for example, would entail assessing the problem objectively, weighing the available options, and selecting the one that best addresses the issue if we came across a challenging circumstance at work. This could entail asking for assistance from coworkers, picking up new abilities, or altering how we approach the current activity. We identify with the Stoic ideal of living by reason when we concentrate on workable answers.

Because it symbolizes our capacity to stay unfazed by life's inevitable changes and uncertainties, adaptability is a crucial virtue in stoic philosophy. Stoics believed that while we have little control over outside forces, we can control our interactions with them. To be flexible is to acknowledge that life is full of change and to be prepared to modify our goals and course of action as necessary.

If we were to lose our job, for instance, we would be able to adjust by accepting the circumstances without giving up. Rather, we would search for fresh opportunities, such as switching careers, getting a new job, or learning new skills. This ability to adapt guarantees that we will always be able to move forward in the face of difficulty, no matter what barriers we come against.

We can gain a better understanding of our responses to different situations by practicing mindfulness in our thoughts and behaviors. Self-awareness enables us to change our direction and take a more

Doing What is Necessary

practical and adaptive posture by helping us identify when we are being rigid or unduly idealistic.

The Stoics placed a strong emphasis on the value of living in the present. Instead of becoming mired down by regrets from the past or worries about the future, we can make better decisions that are pertinent to our current situation by focusing on the here and now.

Recognizing change as a necessary part of life may make us more flexible. We must embrace change as a chance for development and advancement, rather than becoming afraid of it. Although aiming for achievement is vital, we shouldn't grow dependent on certain results. By keeping our attention on our activities rather than the outcomes, we can continue to be flexible and realistic, prepared to modify our efforts as necessary. By constantly acquiring new information and honing our abilities, we can make sure we're ready for any obstacles that come our way. This proactive mindset keeps us adaptable and receptive to new opportunities.

From a Stoic standpoint, being pragmatic and adaptive basically means following reason and embracing life as it comes. It entails concentrating on the things under our control, acting pragmatically, and maintaining our adaptability in the face of change. By developing these traits, we can confidently face life's challenges and preserve our inner serenity while remaining ever-prepared.

Life Like a Warrior

"I will be brave, courageous, and tough."

* * *

The practice of stoicism helps us develop inner fortitude and remain calm in the face of difficulty. We can skillfully and gracefully handle life's obstacles by embracing these virtues. Let's examine what it means to be tough, strong, and brave from a stoic perspective.

According to Stoic philosophy, bravery is not the absence of fear but rather the ability to confront it using reasoned reasoning. Although fear is a normal human emotion, letting it dictate how we behave causes needless misery. Stoicism cautions us to recognize the roots of our fears and handle them with a clear mind. When we realize that several anxieties stem from illogical thoughts or uncontrollable circumstances, we can confront them in a calm and rational manner.

For example, consider dealing with a difficult conversation or a demanding situation at work. A stoic mindset would be admitting that such circumstances could cause worry, but making the decision

Becoming Stoic

to act in accordance with our values despite our fears. This involves mentally preparing ourselves, concentrating on our controllable factors, and graciously accepting the result. We demonstrate true bravery by acting honorably and sensibly, even in the face of fear.

Bravery and courage go hand in hand. Bravery is the ability to continuously uphold our ideals in the face of adversity. It is about following our morals and convictions without wavering in the face of external pressure or potential consequences. According to stoicism, our behavior, particularly while under hardship, defines who we are as a person. Therefore, courage is the resolve to live morally, no matter what.

Consider the example of someone rising up against injustice. The courageous person is not always the one who is fearless; rather, it is the one who chooses to stand up for what they believe in and behave morally in spite of any consequences or danger. This unwavering dedication to morality is the foundation of stoic courage. It entails acknowledging that external factors shouldn't shape our moral compass while remaining steadfast in our commitment to ourselves and our principles.

The Stoic philosophy views toughness as possessing the inner strength and resilience to confront challenges without compromising our moral character or mental health. Life is unpredictable, and adversity is inevitable. Stoicism builds emotional and mental resilience, which equips us to handle these difficulties. This entails understanding that, rather than the events themselves, it is how we react to them that gives us power.

Being tough means acknowledging pain and suffering as natural parts of life and handling them with grace and tenacity. For instance, a stoic individual might concentrate on keeping their inner peace and acting morally while suffering personal loss or failure. They wouldn't let anything outside of themselves control their happiness or sense of value. Rather, they would view these difficulties as chances to practice their philosophy and develop their character.

Bravery, courage, and toughness combined form a powerful

Life Like a Warrior

framework for leading a stoic life. These qualities both support and relate to each other. To face our fears, we need bravery; to act morally, we need courage; and to persevere through difficult times without losing our way, we need toughness.

Living by these principles practically requires consistently engaging in mindfulness and introspection exercises. Through analyzing our thoughts and behaviors, we can pinpoint instances where fear, outside influences, or misfortune may be impacting us. At that point, we can choose to align our actions with our Stoic principles once again. The core of stoic practice is this never-ending process of self-improvement.

Developing perspective and gratitude can also help to support and strengthen these qualities. To maintain a balanced perspective, we must acknowledge the fleeting nature of external situations and be grateful for what we already have. This kind of thinking enables us to maintain our toughness and bravery in the face of life's biggest obstacles.

In conclusion, our dedication to embodying bravery, fortitude, and toughness is evidence of the depth of our character. The tenets of stoicism tell us that real strength comes from inside, from our capacity to face fear, stick to our principles, and rise over hardship with dignity. If we adopt intelligence and virtue, we can lead resilient, meaningful lives.

Pick Your Battles

"I will pick my battles with reason and avoid those that can't be won."

* * *

In life, there are a lot of decisions, conflicts, and challenges that need our attention. These "battles" can take many different forms, including interpersonal conflicts, work difficulties, emotional problems, and societal issues. Stoicism teaches us to thoroughly consider all of our options before choosing to fight, as well as to handle these disagreements calmly and rationally.

To properly select our fights, we must understand the nature of every struggle. This entails posing several questions to ourselves, such as; Is it worthwhile for me to invest time and energy into this battle? What outcomes are possible? Can I control the circumstances or influence how things turn out? By answering these questions, we might be able to gain clarity and decide where to focus our efforts.

Reason is central to the Stoic philosophy. It entails using reason

Becoming Stoic

and clarity of thought as opposed to allowing our emotions or instincts to dictate our actions. When there is a chance of conflict, it is critical to step back and evaluate the situation objectively.

Consider a workplace dispute as an example. Before acting based solely on our emotions, we might use reason to assess the circumstances. What is the primary reason for the dispute? What kind of consequences might joining this battle have? Is there a constructive way to deal with this that doesn't exacerbate it? We can decide if it is better to let things go or to confront the issue head-on in a reasoned manner.

The key to choosing our battles wisely is to recognize which ones we cannot win. Stoicism teaches us to accept our limitations and the things we cannot alter. We cannot win certain conflicts or achieve desirable outcomes, making them pointless to wage.

For instance, it is sometimes impossible to change someone else's strongly held beliefs or behaviors. People are generally averse to change, especially when it impacts essential aspects of who they are. In these circumstances, it makes more sense to accept that we cannot control other people and focus instead on the things within our control, such as our own responses and actions.

Understanding when a struggle is unwinnable aids in preventing unnecessary frustration and rage. After that, we could concentrate on more desirable and achievable goals.

Intelligently selecting our conflicts also entails setting priorities for what matters most. Not every argument or problem is worth our time and effort. Stoicism urges us to focus on what is essential and let go of irrelevant concerns.

In actuality, this may entail choosing to focus our resources on growing as individuals, creating meaningful connections, and having a positive influence on society rather than getting dragged into frivolous disputes or meaningless pursuits. Concentrating on the important things in life can help us lead happier and more purposeful lives.

Among stoicism's main goals are inner serenity and quiet. Fighting unnecessary battles could disturb this calmness and result in

Pick Your Battles

tension and worry. By choosing our battles wisely, we safeguard our emotional and mental health.

When faced with a potential conflict, we can ask ourselves the following question: Will waging this war benefit or hinder my inner peace? If the latter is the answer, it might be better to avoid getting into any arguments at all. This does not imply avoiding all issues; rather, it only means exercising caution in determining which ones demand our time and focus.

It's important to stay out of fights we can't win, but it's also important to prepare ourselves for the ones we do choose to fight. The mental and emotional resources that stoicism provides enable us to mentally and emotionally prepare ourselves for life's challenges and cultivate the courage and perseverance to meet them head-on.

We ensure the focus of our efforts on meaningful and winnable conflicts by strategically choosing our battles. By applying this strategic strategy, we avoid constant fatigue from meaningless activities and instead concentrate on significant challenges that foster our achievement and personal growth.

Retiring from a war is sometimes the best line of action. This is an indication of strategic thought rather than weakness. Knowing when to give up can help us avoid unnecessary losses and conserve our resources. It also provides us with an opportunity to collect ourselves, reconsider our approach, and potentially devise a new one.

For example, choosing to back off from an intense argument and bring it up later, after the tension has decreased, can lead to a more amicable and productive discussion. Strategic retreat can be a very useful tool for maintaining relationships and achieving long-term goals.

To sum up, choosing our battles wisely and avoiding those that are unwinnable is a sensible strategy based on Stoic philosophy. By focusing on the important things in life, acknowledging when a disagreement is unwinnable, maintaining inner peace, and acting with reason, we can lead more vigorous and joyful lives. This tactical plan will enable us to concentrate our efforts on the most important

Becoming Stoic

challenges, strengthen our resilience and flexibility, and more clearly and purposefully achieve our goals. With careful judgment and strategic thought, we can navigate life's challenges with grace and wisdom, leading to a more meaningful and satisfied existence in the end.

Wisdom from Any Source

"I will look for wisdom, no matter where it comes from, if it stands up to reason and makes my life better."

* * *

A key principle of Stoic philosophy is the search for knowledge and truth via logical reasoning with practical application. According to Stoicism, wisdom is the cornerstone of a good and happy life and can originate from a variety of sources as long as it is reasonable and beneficial.

First and foremost, wisdom means knowing ourselves and the world. It involves making wise choices based on information and expertise. Wisdom, according to the Stoics, is not limited to any one person, text, or custom. Instead, one can discover wisdom in everyday interactions, diverse cultural viewpoints, and diverse concepts. The secret is to examine each source critically and with an open mind, determining its applicability and reasonableness.

When we declare that we will seek wisdom from all sources, we are admitting that sometimes the most unexpected sources can yield insightful information. A discussion with a buddy, a book on a new topic, or even a trying situation can teach us something valuable. The stoic philosophy promotes lifelong learning, curiosity, and an open mind to new concepts that can advance human development.

The principle's second clause, "if it stands up to reason," highlights the significance of reasoned reasoning. Stoicism regards reason as the highest human faculty. It enables us to recognize what is real, honorable, and beneficial. Before accepting a piece of knowledge, we should consider its logic, data support, and alignment with our worldview. By following reason as our guide, we can avoid succumbing to erroneous assumptions, superstitions, or emotional inclinations.

For example, we should carefully consider advice that recommends significant life changes based on personal experience. We ought to weigh the data, contemplate the possible outcomes, and decide if it is consistent with our values and objectives. This logical assessment allows us to make more informed decisions with better results.

The final line of the principle, "and makes my life better," underscores the practical application of wisdom in everyday situations. A practical philosophy, stoicism aims to make our lives better by encouraging virtue and reasoned behavior. Putting wisdom into practice improves our relationships, general well-being, and standard of living, surpassing mere academic knowledge.

To give an example, consider picking up a new stress-reduction strategy. If this method calms us down and increases our focus while standing up against logic and proof, it's a priceless pearl of wisdom. By using it regularly, we can enhance our productivity and mental well-being, which will enhance our quality of life.

The Stoic tradition views the search for wisdom as an ongoing journey. We constantly strive to increase, develop, and improve our comprehension. This entails being willing to adjust our opinions in response to fresh information or persuasive arguments. It also entails

Wisdom from Any Source

accepting that there is always space for growth and that we do not always have the answers.

Moreover, humility is a necessary component of a knowledge quest. It is essential that we accept our limitations and remain open to gaining knowledge from people, irrespective of their status or origin. Anyone can share wisdom, so we should listen to everyone. This transparency promotes a climate of respect for one another and ongoing education.

In reality, pursuing wisdom can take many different forms. We can learn new things through reading a variety of literature, having meaningful conversations, thinking back on our experiences, and getting input from others. It also entails challenging our presumptions and being prepared to modify our opinions and actions in light of fresh information.

In summary, a core Stoic principle is the resolve to seek wisdom regardless of its source, as long as it is consistent with reason and improves our lives. It motivates us to pursue knowledge and self-improvement with an open mind, reason, and practicality. We develop a more contented, moral, and enlightened life by appreciating reason and seeking wisdom that truly improves our lives. This method helps society become wiser and more harmonious, in addition to benefiting each of us personally.

Chapter 9
FORTITUDE and RESILIENCE

Face It Fearlessly

"I will "let come what may" and have no problems or concerns."

* * *

Stoicism teaches us to distinguish between our controllable and uncontrollable life events. We have no influence over the outside world, others' actions, or the unavoidable changes that come with living. We do, however, have power over our own attitudes, ideas, and reactions. By focusing on what we can control and accepting what we cannot, we can maintain our inner peace and minimize unnecessary stress and concern.

Imagine yourself in a situation where plans suddenly change. Perhaps you have to postpone a much-anticipated event or lose an employment opportunity. A stoic person would remind himself that these outside circumstances are beyond their control rather than responding with annoyance or fear. We relieve ourselves of needless mental and emotional strain by letting go of the need to influence these results and accepting them as they are.

Becoming Stoic

By practicing mindfulness and presence, one can practically adopt this stoic style of thinking. By living in the present moment to its fullest, we can better embrace what is happening, free from ideas of how things "should" be. By practicing mindfulness, we can examine our thoughts and feelings more objectively, allowing us to respond calmly and clearly to life's challenges. For instance, you can practice mindfulness by taking deep breaths and paying attention to your environment if you are late and caught in traffic, rather than losing your cool. This aids in maintaining your composure and accepting things as they are.

Accepting the idea of impermanence is a key component of the Stoic method. Nothing in life is permanent, and things change all the time. Recognizing this reality allows us to let go of our attachment to certain results and flow with life's natural rhythm. This does not mean we become apathetic or inactive; rather, we remain proactive and involved while accepting that we cannot control everything. For example, when a personal relationship ends or changes, we can choose to embrace it as a normal part of life's journey and concentrate on the chance for personal development and novel experiences rather than holding onto the past or fighting the change.

Another thing that stoicism teaches us is to reframe the way we see obstacles and challenges. We might perceive them as chances for learning and development rather than as issues. Every obstacle we encounter offers us the opportunity to put our virtues—like courage, patience, and wisdom—into practice. By adopting this viewpoint, we can face challenges with resilience and interest instead of dread and annoyance. For instance, if you come across a challenging project at work, you should see it as a chance to showcase your strengths and advance your skills rather than give up.

Engaging in gratitude practices is another effective strategy for sustaining a stoic mindset. We can change our perspective from what is lacking to what is abundant in our lives by taking time each day to think about the things for which we are thankful. This optimistic

Face It Fearlessly

outlook lessens our propensity to worry about the future or focus on the past and encourages us to enjoy the present. One way to develop an attitude of thankfulness and contentment even in the face of difficulties is to write down a few items each day in your gratitude diary.

Understanding the need for acceptance in managing emotions is also crucial. Stoicism teaches us to accept our emotions as normal reactions to the things that happen in life, rather than to control or deny them. We may react to events more deliberately and carefully when we acknowledge our emotions without letting them rule us. After acknowledging and understanding your depression or disappointment, you can treat it constructively.

The Stoic technique of "negative visualization" can also assist us in accepting and preparing for life's uncertainties. We can develop resilience and lessen our fear of the unknown by mentally practicing how we would respond to potential obstacles or setbacks. Because we have already acknowledged and accepted the likelihood of such situations, this exercise aids us in remaining calm and grounded when we encounter real difficulties.

Ultimately, the preservation of inner calm depends on leading a purposeful life and acting in accordance with our moral principles. We can live more meaningful and satisfying lives if we focus our attention on the things that really matter to us and let go of unimportant worries. This means choosing wisely, not giving in to transient cravings or outside pressure, and acting in accordance with our values and priorities. For instance, rather than pursuing financial success or social acceptance, you might place a higher priority on spending time with loved ones and improving the lives of others if you value your family and community.

In conclusion, embracing the "let come what may" mentality and letting go of all worries and issues is a profound and freeing discipline that has its roots in Stoic philosophy. We can develop inner calm and resilience by concentrating on what we can control, engaging in mindfulness and gratitude practices, accepting impermanence,

Becoming Stoic

rephrasing difficulties, accepting emotions, being ready for uncertainty, and leading purposeful lives. By guiding us through the intricacies of life with composure and clarity, this method promotes happiness and fulfillment. By studying the ageless lessons of stoicism, we can learn to accept and value life as it happens, maintain our inner equilibrium, and approach the journey with grace and wisdom.

It All Makes Me Stronger

> "I will live by the motto;
> What does not kill me makes me stronger."

* * *

Stoicism teaches that life is filled with obstacles and difficulties, and our responses to these challenges shape our character and resilience. By adopting this motto, we embrace the idea that facing and overcoming hardships makes us stronger individuals.

Stoicism places a strong emphasis on viewing obstacles as chances for development rather than as failures. Difficulties provide us with the opportunity to grow in traits like bravery, patience, and wisdom. We develop resilience and inner strength every time we face and solve a challenge. For example, you can grow both personally and professionally if you tackle a challenging circumstance at work with a positive attitude and a drive to learn and improve, such as a tough project or a fight with a colleague.

Stoicism emphasizes distinguishing between controllable and uncontrollable factors. Thoughts, attitudes, and reactions are things

Becoming Stoic

we can control; external events and other people's acts are beyond our control. By concentrating on our sphere of influence, we enable ourselves to overcome hardship with greater efficacy. When confronted with a difficult circumstance, we have the option to view it as a chance to put our morals into practice and fortify our character. For example, if you go through a personal loss, such as a relationship breakup or the passing of a loved one, you may get through the grief and come out stronger if you pay attention to how you react and look for opportunities to learn from the experience.

Resilience is another skill that comes from living by the maxim, "What does not kill me makes me stronger." Resilience is the ability to overcome obstacles and adapt to change. In order to develop resilience, we must confront and tolerate discomfort, since it is only by overcoming adversity that we grow stronger and more capable. For example, you can turn a negative experience into a positive one by seeing a big setback—like losing your job—as a chance to learn new skills, consider alternative career routes, and strengthen your resilience.

Stoicism teaches the importance of accepting and appreciating reality as it is. Life is unpredictable and frequently out of our control. Accepting this fact allows us to concentrate on how we handle the difficulties in life. Acceptance entails acknowledging the circumstances and acting constructively, not giving up or becoming passive. Acknowledging the truth about your chronic illness, focusing on effective management strategies, seeking treatment, and maintaining a positive mindset can facilitate the building of strength and resilience.

The concept of changing the way we view obstacles is another important component of this phrase. We can view difficulties as opportunities for personal development, rather than as threats. Reframing entails altering our perspective on and analysis of various circumstances. For example, if you experience a financial setback, you can choose to consider it a chance to learn more about money management, create new investment and saving plans, and strengthen your financial resilience.

Stoicism's other potent weapon that fits with this maxim is practicing thankfulness. We can change our perspective from what we lack to what we have by routinely reflecting on the things for which we are grateful. This optimistic outlook supports us in developing resilience and keeping a sense of contentment even in the face of difficulties. If you are going through a tough moment, for instance, spending a few minutes every day thinking about the things you have to be grateful for —like encouraging friends, a stunning sunset, or accomplishments in your life—can help you stay optimistic and gain resilience.

Additionally, stoicism emphasizes the value of ongoing introspection and self-improvement. Through consistent introspection and self-reflection, we can pinpoint our areas of weakness and strive to improve ourselves as people. In order to continue improving ourselves, we must meet obstacles head-on. For instance, you can concentrate on being more patient and composed if you know that you often respond with rage or annoyance in particular circumstances. This will help you see every difficult scenario as a chance for personal development.

Creating a support system is another crucial aspect of adhering to this slogan. Although stoicism places a strong emphasis on personal accountability, it also recognizes the need for support and community. Having a helpful and like-minded support system around us can help us overcome obstacles and develop resilience. For instance, getting advice from a mentor, joining a support group, or maintaining relationships with friends and family can provide us with the fortitude and inspiration we need to go through challenges.

Living a stoic lifestyle can help us live up to the proverb, "What does not kill me makes me stronger." This could entail scheduling daily time for thankfulness, introspection, and mindfulness. Establishing a morning routine that incorporates journaling, meditation, and intention-setting, for example, can help you develop mental and

Becoming Stoic

emotional resilience and get ready to confront life's obstacles with poise and fortitude.

Ultimately, according to the maxim "What does not kill me makes me stronger," this is consistent with the basic ideas of Stoic philosophy. We can develop the inner strength and wisdom necessary to overcome life's obstacles by accepting challenges as opportunities for growth, concentrating on what we can control, developing resilience, accepting reality, changing our perspective, practicing gratitude, reflecting on ourselves, and creating a support system. We can exemplify the actual meaning of Stoic philosophy by transforming obstacles into opportunities for personal growth and advancement through constant practice and dedication to these ideals.

Training for Crisis

"I will train myself to deal with crisis before it is occurring."

* * *

By preparing our minds and spirits for life's inevitable obstacles, stoicism helps us face them with courage and composure. When a crisis arises, we can handle it better if we anticipate it and prepare for it. Building a support network, practicing mental rehearsal, developing resilience, and concentrating on our controllables are some of the fundamental techniques of this strategy.

First of all, mental practice is an effective way to get ready for emergencies. This is about picturing possible obstacles and figuring out how you would coolly and collectedly face them. Through mental practice, you can create a mental model for handling circumstances that arise in real life. You can imagine your reaction if you were worried about losing your job. Consider the actions you would take, such as applying for new jobs, updating your resume, and contacting contacts. Because it provides you with a sense of control and preparedness, this mental rehearsal aids in the reduction of fear and anxiety.

Building resilience is a crucial part of crisis preparedness. The capacity to overcome hardship and preserve stability and hope is known as resilience. Developing resilience entails improving your physical, mental, and emotional well-being. Regular exercise, eating a balanced diet, getting adequate sleep, and engaging in mindfulness or meditation practices can all help you achieve this. These practices not only enhance your general health but also provide you with the stamina and mental clarity you need to overcome obstacles. For example, engaging in regular physical activity can improve your mood and reduce stress, enabling you to better handle challenging circumstances.

Focusing on what you can control and accepting what you cannot are two other key tenets of stoicism. Natural disasters, economic downturns, and other events beyond our control are just a few examples of the uncontrollable factors that play a role in many crises. Focusing on your own behaviors, ideas, and dispositions will help you stay in control and lessen your sense of powerlessness. For instance, you might not be able to affect the economy during a financial crisis, but you still have power over your spending, saving, and resource management practices. It keeps you proactive and grounded, allowing you to concentrate on things that are under your control.

Creating a network of support is another essential component of crisis preparedness. In difficult circumstances, it is vital to have a network of friends, family, or mentors who can provide direction, support, and encouragement. These connections give you a feeling of belonging and serve as a constant reminder that you are not alone. For example, seeking the advice of a trustworthy friend or counselor during a personal crisis can help you process your feelings and see things from a different angle. Building solid relationships gives you a safety net that gets you through challenging times.

Continuing education and skill building is another useful strategy for crisis preparedness. Gaining additional information and

Training for Crisis

skills over time makes you more adaptive and resourceful. This could include picking up a new pastime, developing new job abilities, or keeping up with trends and current events. For instance, if you are concerned about the stability of your work, investigating alternative career paths or picking up new skills related to your industry can help you become more adaptable and better equipped to handle future changes. Taking the initiative increases your self-assurance and prepares you to take on unforeseen obstacles.

Stoicism also emphasizes the value of remaining composed and sensible in the face of adversity. This entails learning emotional self-control and resisting the urge to act out of fear or terror. Engaging in mindfulness exercises like meditation or deep breathing exercises is one way to build this skill. These methods support you in maintaining your composure under pressure. For example, taking a few minutes to clear your thoughts and breathe deeply can help you think more clearly and make better decisions if you find yourself in a crisis.

Preparing for crises often involves thinking back on the past and applying what you've learned. You can determine what was successful and what needs improvement by reviewing how you previously dealt with difficulties. This thought strengthens your problem-solving skills and expands your repertoire of useful tactics. If you have experienced a health crisis in the past, for instance, think back on the actions you took to handle it, the resources you found useful, and how you can use these lessons in other situations. This ongoing learning process improves your ability to handle new difficulties.

Fortifying yourself against catastrophes might also involve cultivating an optimistic and grateful outlook. To be grateful is to acknowledge and value the good things in your life, especially when you are facing hardship. By encouraging a positive mindset, this exercise helps you change your attention from what is going wrong to what is going right. Optimism means believing that you can overcome obstacles and holding on to hope. For example, if you are going through a personal crisis, you can increase your resilience and morale by setting aside some time each day to express your gratitude for

Becoming Stoic

things like your health, your supporting relationships, or your accomplishments.

Having a flexible and adaptive strategy is necessary for successfully managing emergencies. Since life is unpredictable, it can be stressful and frustrating to strictly adhere to schedules or expectations. By practicing flexibility, you can respond creatively and easily to changing conditions. This entails keeping an open mind, considering other approaches, and viewing change as a chance for personal development. For instance, instead of giving up when a catastrophe derails your plans, search for new avenues that may yield unanticipated advantages or find substitutes for achieving your objectives.

In conclusion, a key component of stoic philosophy is learning how to handle crises before they happen. You can develop the strength and readiness required to face life's challenges with confidence and composure by engaging in mental rehearsal, developing resilience, concentrating on what you can control, creating a support system, learning continuously, keeping a calm and collected mindset, thinking back on previous experiences, encouraging gratitude and optimism, and embracing adaptability. You can develop an unbreakable mentality by embodying the true spirit of stoicism and living a resilient, inner-peaceful existence by regularly practicing and adhering to these principles.

Mentally Solid

"I will be prepared and mentally solid for all hard events that come into my life."

* * *

Stoicism teaches that while we cannot control external events, we can control our responses to them. Through mental preparation and character building, we can face challenges with poise and elegance. This strategy includes a number of key practices, including preparing for obstacles, acknowledging that suffering will inevitably occur, focusing on our controllable actions, developing inner virtues, and upholding a constant improvement mindset.

Being able to anticipate challenges is one of the most important aspects of being ready for life's obstacles. *Premeditatio malorum*, or premeditation of evils, is a technique that Stoics frequently supported. This exercise entails imagining possible obstacles and thinking through possible solutions. When we prepare for potential challenges, we experience less shock or overwhelm when they arise. For instance, if we know that we might lose our job, we might psycho-

Becoming Stoic

logically get ready to deal with it cooly and strategically. By practicing mentally, we may strengthen our resilience and maintain our composure in the face of difficulty.

Recognizing that hardship is a reality is another crucial habit. Because of the nature of life, the human experience is inevitably filled with obstacles and uncertainty. Recognizing this fact allows us to release ourselves from the irrational assumption that life should always be easy and trouble-free. Rather, we cultivate a mindset that sees obstacles as chances for improvement and education. For example, acknowledging a personal setback as a normal part of life enables us to concentrate on how we can get past it and come out stronger. This acceptance fosters resilience and inner serenity.

Focusing on what we can control is a basic tenet of stoicism that helps us prepare for difficult situations. Although we can't change the world, we can change our thoughts, actions, and beliefs. We give ourselves the capacity to overcome obstacles by focusing our efforts on the things we can control. In a difficult relationship, we can neither control nor change the other person's behavior, but we can control our reaction and choose to be patient and understanding. This emphasis on internal control aids in our ability to remain composed and act honorably when faced with challenges.

Building mental fortitude also requires the cultivation of inner values. Stoicism emphasizes the value of characteristics like wisdom, courage, justice, and temperance. These qualities act as pillars that support us in making morally sound decisions. Living according to these ideals gives us a solid moral foundation that helps us through difficult times. For instance, depending on the virtue of wisdom can assist us in making a deliberate and conscientious choice when presented with a moral conundrum. This moral strategy not only fortifies our character but also improves our capacity to meet life's obstacles with dignity.

Keeping an attitude of constant improvement is another important habit. The stoic perspective urges us to see life as a journey of self-improvement. Through a dedication to continuous education and

Mentally Solid

personal growth, we can acquire the abilities and understanding required to effectively handle obstacles. To help us evolve and adjust to changing circumstances, we might, for instance, set personal goals, regularly reflect on our experiences, and ask for feedback. This constant state of improvement builds resilience and equips us to confidently take on new difficulties.

We must also develop self-discipline for mental stability. Controlling our impulses and adhering to our principles and objectives are two aspects of self-discipline. Self-control exercises help us develop the mental toughness required to resist outside influences. For example, self-control in areas like food, exercise, and sleep is necessary to sustain a healthy lifestyle. By concentrating on these areas of our lives, we take charge of our health and establish a solid inner base that carries us through difficult times.

Mindfulness is another useful technique for mentally getting ready for challenging situations. Being mindful entails paying close attention to the present and evaluating our thoughts and emotions objectively. This activity allows us to better understand our internal states and how they affect our behavior. By practicing mindfulness, we can better control how we respond to outside events and maintain our attention on the things we can control. For instance, mindfulness enables us to resist the need to respond rashly in stressful situations by pausing, taking a deep breath, and selecting a composed and logical response.

Regular self-reflection is also necessary to develop mental stability. Through consistent self-evaluation of our behaviors and ideas, we can pinpoint opportunities for development and draw lessons from past mistakes. This reflection allows us to learn more about ourselves and advance in our own development. For example, journaling about our everyday events, feelings, and ideas can give us important insights into our inner selves. With time, this exercise can assist us in seeing patterns, creating more effective coping mechanisms, and strengthening our inner resilience.

Developing thankfulness is another crucial habit. Practicing grati-

Becoming Stoic

tude entails taking time to reflect on the good things in our lives and to be grateful for what we already have. This practice cultivates an abundance attitude as opposed to a scarcity mindset and aids in maintaining a balanced outlook. We might develop a sense of resilience and satisfaction that protects us from outside disruptions by concentrating on the things for which we are thankful. For example, it can improve our general well-being and strengthen our inner strength to take a moment each day to reflect on the things we have to be thankful for, such as our health, relationships, or accomplishments in life.

In conclusion, a core tenet of Stoic philosophy is being ready and psychologically strong for all difficult situations that arise in our lives. We can develop a resilient and composed mindset by being aware of impending challenges, accepting that hardship is a reality, concentrating on what we can control, cultivating inner virtues, keeping a mindset of continuous improvement, developing self-discipline, practicing mindfulness, regularly reflecting on our lives, and cultivating gratitude. This strategy not only makes it easier for us to overcome obstacles in life, but it also promotes inner contentment and serenity. By putting these techniques into reality, we can live resilient, moral lives and truly embody the core of Stoic philosophy.

Strong At All Times

"I will control my mind to remain strong regardless of physical violence, victimization, injustice, or all kinds of adversity."

* * *

Life often presents us with difficult situations—whether it be physical violence, victimization, injustice, or other forms of adversity. These challenges can test our resilience and inner strength. However, by focusing on our mental fortitude, we can choose how we respond to these situations and remain steadfast in our values and principles.

One practical way to apply this principle is to cultivate a mindset of inner strength and resilience. This involves regularly reflecting on our values and beliefs and reinforcing our commitment to them. For example, if we value justice and integrity, we can remind ourselves of these principles when faced with injustice or victimization. By anchoring ourselves in our core values, we can maintain our sense of purpose and direction, even in the midst of adversity.

Becoming Stoic

Mindfulness and meditation are also effective tools for maintaining mental strength. These practices help us develop greater awareness of our thoughts and emotions and enable us to respond to challenges with greater clarity and composure. For instance, mindfulness can help us remain grounded and calm in the face of physical violence or victimization, enabling us to think clearly and make rational decisions. Meditation can also provide a sense of inner peace and resilience, helping us cope with stress and adversity more effectively.

The Stoics teach us to distinguish between what we can and cannot control. By focusing on what is within our control—our thoughts, attitudes, and actions—we can avoid feeling overwhelmed by external events. For example, while we cannot control others' actions or the occurrence of injustices, we can control how we respond to them. Instead of letting anger or despair consume us, we can choose to respond with dignity, courage, and compassion.

Developing emotional resilience is another important aspect of this principle. Emotional resilience involves building the capacity to recover quickly from setbacks and adapt to change. This requires self-awareness, emotional regulation, and a proactive approach to personal growth. For example, if we experience an injustice or a traumatic event, we can focus on finding constructive ways to cope and heal, such as seeking support from loved ones, engaging in therapeutic activities, or practicing self-care. By prioritizing our emotional well-being, we can strengthen our ability to face adversity with resilience and grace.

Practicing gratitude and focusing on the positive aspects of our lives can also help us maintain mental strength in the face of adversity. Gratitude involves recognizing and appreciating the beneficial things we have, even in difficult times. For example, if we are dealing with a challenging situation, we can remind ourselves of the support we receive from friends and family, the progress we have made, or the small joys we experience each day. By cultivating an attitude of gratitude, we can shift our focus from what we lack to what we have, fostering a sense of contentment and resilience.

Stoicism also emphasizes the importance of accepting the reality of our circumstances. Acceptance does not mean resignation or passivity; rather, it involves acknowledging the truth of a situation and finding constructive ways to respond. For example, if we face physical violence or victimization, accepting the reality of the situation allows us to take appropriate actions, such as seeking help, protecting ourselves, or advocating for justice. Acceptance helps us stay grounded and focused, enabling us to navigate adversity with clarity and purpose.

Building a supportive network of relationships is another essential aspect of maintaining mental strength. Connecting with others who share our values and offer encouragement can provide a source of strength and perspective. For example, sharing our challenges and successes with trusted friends or family members can help us gain new insights and feel less isolated. A strong support network can provide practical advice, emotional support, and a sense of community, all of which contribute to our overall well-being.

Engaging in regular physical and mental training can also help us build resilience and maintain our inner strength. Physical training, such as exercise or martial arts, can enhance our physical and mental stamina, preparing us to face physical challenges with confidence. Mental training, such as studying philosophy, practicing critical thinking, or engaging in problem-solving activities, can sharpen our cognitive skills and enhance our ability to navigate complex situations. By prioritizing both physical and mental training, we can build a strong foundation for resilience and adaptability.

In conclusion, controlling our minds to remain strong regardless of physical violence, victimization, injustice, or all kinds of adversity is a core Stoic principle that empowers us to navigate life's challenges with resilience and grace. By cultivating a mindset of inner strength and resilience, practicing mindfulness and meditation, distinguishing between what we can control and what we cannot, developing

Becoming Stoic

emotional resilience, practicing gratitude, accepting the reality of our circumstances, building a supportive network, and engaging in regular physical and mental training, we can maintain our inner peace and integrity in the face of adversity. Stoicism teaches us that true strength comes from within, and by focusing on our mental fortitude, we can face life's challenges with courage and composure.

Chapter 10
VIRTUE and KINDNESS

Let Them Shine

"I will let my virtues of truth, justice, and self-control shine from this point forward."

* * *

Stoicism emphasizes the importance of virtues in leading a fulfilling life. By embracing qualities like honesty, fairness, and self-discipline, we can tackle life's obstacles with integrity and wisdom. This essay will delve into ways to nurture and demonstrate these virtues in our day-to-day experiences, using language and real-life scenarios.

Let's start by exploring the virtue of honesty. Living truthfully involves being sincere with ourselves and others. It means speaking the truth when it's hard, and aligning our actions with our principles. Honesty fosters. Genuineness in our interactions lays the groundwork for our behavior. For instance, in an environment where honesty might entail owning up to mistakes rather than trying to hide them, this transparency does not help us learn from our missteps. It also earns us the respect of our peers.

Developing the virtue of honesty also entails pursuing knowledge

Becoming Stoic

and insight. It calls for an approach and a willingness to challenge our assumptions. By aiming to comprehend reality as it's intended to be, we can make sounder and more logical choices.

When we encounter an issue, taking the time to gather information and consider various viewpoints can help us find a better solution.

The next important virtue is justice. In philosophy, justice involves treating others respectfully, acknowledging the value of each person, and acting in ways that benefit everyone. Practicing justice means showing compassion and empathy, speaking out against injustice, and supporting those in need. For instance, when we witness unfair treatment of someone at work or in our community, we can practice justice by advocating for them or providing assistance.

Justice also entails fulfilling our duties and promises. This requires being trustworthy and reliable in our actions. After a difficult commitment to a friend or coworker, we must follow through. By honoring our obligations, we show respect for others and contribute to a peaceful society.

The third virtue to consider is self-control. Self-control, also known as temperance, involves managing our emotions and impulses by practicing restraint and moderation when faced with temptations.

Practicing self-restraint is key to maintaining peace within ourselves and avoiding actions that could cause harm to us or others. For instance, when we feel upset or irritated, practicing self-control involves pausing to calm down and think before responding, which prevents us from saying or doing things we might regret later.

Fostering self-discipline also means being aware of our habits and behaviors, as well as making decisions about how we spend our time and energy. If our aim is to enhance our well-being, exercising self-control may entail opting for food options and committing to physical activity. We can reach our goals by staying focused on our actions. Lead a harmonious life.

Moving forward with these values requires a dedication to

growth and introspection. This entails assessing our decisions and behaviors to ensure they align with our principles. For example, setting aside time each day for reflection on how we have acted with restraint allows us to pinpoint areas where we can improve and actively work towards bettering ourselves.

Setting an example through actions is another crucial element.

When we uphold values like honesty, fairness, and self-discipline, we inspire those around us to follow suit. Our actions can positively impact those in our circle, encouraging a culture of goodness within our communities. For example, by showing integrity and sincerity in the workplace, we can foster an environment of openness and trust among our peers.

It's also beneficial to connect with others who share our dedication to living. Building relationships with individuals can offer encouragement and support. For instance, joining a group or community focused on growth and ethical behavior can lead to discussions and shared experiences that reinforce our commitment to virtue.

Finally, it's important to understand that leading a life is a process. Despite facing obstacles and setbacks along the way, maintaining dedication and resilience is key. Practicing patience and forgiveness towards ourselves and others is crucial. For example, when we don't meet our standards and view it as a chance for growth, a failure can be transformative.

In summary, committing to living a fulfilling life involves showcasing our values of honesty, fairness, and restraint. Adopting the truth fosters trust and authenticity, while implementing justice positively impacts society. Exercising self-control maintains inner peace. By improving ourselves, setting an example, seeking help when needed, and acknowledging that personal growth is an ongoing process, we can embody these values and make a positive impact on our lives and those around us. Stoicism reminds us that strength and fulfillment stem from within, guiding us to navigate life's trials with wisdom.

Good for the Whole

"I will focus on understanding that what is good for the whole is good for the individual."

*　*　*

People believe that humans naturally gravitate toward interactions and flourish in environments that foster cooperation and support. By contributing to the well-being of others, we play a role in creating a community where everyone, including ourselves, can grow and prosper.

Empathy and compassion serve as tools for embracing this belief. When we take the time to understand others perspectives and needs, we do not strengthen our connections. Also cultivate a sense of unity. For instance, offering assistance to a struggling colleague can ease their burden. Enhance the work atmosphere. This collaborative spirit contributes to a team dynamic that benefits all involved.

Furthermore, prioritizing the good encourages us to act with honesty and fairness. Considerations for others' welfare guide our decisions, fostering trust and mutual respect within our circles. For example, a business leader who guarantees pay and safe working conditions creates an environment for employees. This commitment does not enhance the well-being of the workforce. It also bolsters the company's standing in the industry, benefiting both employees and leadership.

Another key aspect of this principle involves exercising self-control and moderation. By tempering our desires and focusing on what matters, we avoid actions that could potentially harm the community.

For instance, by being mindful of our consumption habits and reducing waste, we can help conserve resources for the future. This not only promotes well-being but also ensures that essential resources remain accessible to us and future generations.

Stoicism emphasizes that true happiness and contentment stem from within rather than relying on material possessions or social status. By aligning our aspirations with the good, we can attain a profound sense of purpose and fulfillment. For example, engaging in volunteer work for a cause we're passionate about can bring satisfaction as we contribute positively to the welfare of others.

Furthermore, recognizing that what benefits society as a whole also serves individual interests can guide us in resolving conflicts. Prioritizing the good encourages us to seek solutions that cater to everyone's needs rather than solely focusing on personal gain. In situations like community resource disputes, striving for a distribution fosters harmony and minimizes potential tensions.

This principle also underscores the importance of taking accountability for our actions and their repercussions on others. Acknowledging that our decisions impact communal well-being motivates us to act compassionately towards others. For example, by being mindful of our impact on the environment and choosing practices, we can play a role in addressing climate change, which benefits not only our surroundings but also the well-being of future generations.

In addition to advocating for structural changes that promote the greater good, another way to embody this Stoic philosophy is through

Good for the Whole

action. Supporting policies and actions that tackle injustices safeguards the environment. Ensure access to education and healthcare, which can contribute to creating a fairer and more inclusive society. Working towards these objectives enhances the welfare of our community, fostering a living environment for ourselves and those we care about.

Moreover, embracing this principle can cultivate a sense of peace and resilience within us. Recognizing the interconnection between our well-being. Understanding the interconnection between our well-being and that of others allows us to let go of excessive self-centeredness and ego. This shift enables us to focus on what holds value in life while staying grounded amidst adversity. For instance, in times of crisis, prioritizing community needs fosters unity and collective empowerment, enabling us to navigate challenges with increased fortitude.

Ultimately, acknowledging that what benefits the collective good also serves individual interests aligns us with nature's harmony and echoes the belief in living in harmony with principles. This involves understanding our place in the universe and behaving in accordance with it. By doing so, we foster a sense of connection and purpose, acknowledging that our choices are impacting the world around us.

To sum up, focusing on the idea that what benefits society as a whole also benefits each individual is a principle of Stoicism that can positively change our lives and communities. We can lead a more balanced and meaningful life by showing empathy and kindness, acting with honesty and fairness, practicing self-control and moderation, aligning our aspirations with ethical conflict resolution, constructively owning up to our actions, advocating for social progress, and embracing natural order. Stoicism teaches us that prioritizing the welfare of others ultimately benefits ourselves too, leading to a more interconnected existence.

Giving Back Love

"I will give back love to anyone that gives it to me."

* * *

Understanding the Stoic perspective on emotions, known as "passions," is crucial. Stoicism doesn't promote suppressing all emotions. Stoicism prioritizes the cultivation of positive, rational emotions that contribute to a life filled with virtue. People view love, when rooted in reason and virtue, as an emotion that fosters comprehension, empathy, and solidarity among people. Therefore, reciprocating love isn't an exchange but a reinforcement of upright social connections.

To effectively reciprocate love, it's important to grasp the meaning of love. It goes beyond affection and encompasses acts of kindness, understanding, support, and reverence for others dignity. For example, if someone demonstrates love by supporting us in times of need, reciprocating that love could mean offering support when they encounter difficulties.

Furthermore, Stoicism intertwines the concept of empathy with

Becoming Stoic

the practice of returning love. Empathy entails comprehending and sharing others feelings. By cultivating empathy, we become more sensitive to the emotions and needs of those around us, facilitating expressions of love in return.

For example, when a friend demonstrates love by listening to our worries, we reciprocate by offering an attentive ear when they seek to confide.

Practicing gratitude plays a role in reciprocating love. Stoicism guides us to be grateful for aspects of our lives, including the love displayed by others. Recognizing and expressing appreciation for this affection strengthens our relationships in a positive way. We encourage a reciprocal exchange of care and support. This may include expressing gratitude to those who show us love and acknowledging how their actions enrich our lives.

Moreover, reciprocating love entails being fully present and attentive during interactions. In the hustle and bustle of life, it's common to overlook the kindness of others. In order to genuinely reciprocate love, we must fully engage in our interactions, demonstrating our value and cherished nature to others. This requires participating in conversations, listening attentively, and responding to their needs and feelings with empathy.

Returning love also involves behaving with honesty and reliability. Love is not about gestures; it thrives on consistent, small acts of kindness and thoughtfulness. This could involve carrying out acts of kindness for others, like offering unprompted assistance with tasks or consistently providing support when someone is in need.

Stoicism underscores the importance of community and the conviction that we share a connection with something beyond ourselves. Within this framework, reciprocating love involves enhancing the welfare of our community. This may entail volunteering, backing community initiatives, or simply carrying out acts of kindness that enhance the atmosphere.

Nevertheless, it's crucial to understand that while Stoicism promotes giving back love, it also instructs us to steer clear of relying

Giving Back Love

heavily on external approval. Our sense of self-worth should ideally stem from our judgment and virtuous conduct rather than seeking validation or affection from others. Striking this balance enables us to cultivate beneficial relationships without becoming excessively reliant on them for our happiness and self-assurance.

In some ways, committing to "return love to those who show it to me" embodies principles. It underscores the importance of nurturing connections, displaying empathy, practicing appreciation, being present in interactions, and behaving consistently. These actions do not fortify our bonds with others. Our actions also cultivate a community that is more supportive and compassionate. Through consistent acts of reciprocating love, we exemplify the notion of leading a virtuous life that aligns personal well-being with the greater good. This method not only enhances our existence. It also creates a more interconnected world.

The Higher Standard

"I will always hold myself to a higher standard."

* * *

To begin with, let's clarify what it means to hold oneself to a standard through a lens. It entails setting and working towards objectives, especially in areas related to ethical behavior and character growth. It goes beyond achievements like career success or social standing; instead, it focuses on nurturing virtues such as wisdom, justice, courage, and moderation. By aspiring to embody these virtues, individuals aim not only to live but also to live honorably.

The practice of holding oneself accountable commences with self-awareness—understanding one's strengths and weaknesses, motivations, and impulses. Stoicism advocates for self-examination to assess one's actions and choices against the benchmark of virtue. For example, at the end of each day, one may reflect on the day's events. Think about whether their actions were truly just or if wisdom guided their decisions.

Self-assessment assists us in pinpointing areas where we might

Becoming Stoic

fall short of our expectations and devising strategies for future improvement.

Maintaining standards requires self-discipline. It entails controlling our impulses and desires, which can lead us astray from our behavior. For example, we might choose to wake up early for meditation or study, even when we feel like sleeping in, because we value growth and mental clarity. It might also mean turning down invitations to gatherings because we prioritize moderation and making productive use of our time. Self-discipline is not about restricting ourselves but about making decisions that align better with our values and long-term objectives.

Courage is another aspect of upholding standards. It often entails facing truths about ourselves or stepping out of our comfort zones to evolve and develop. This could involve challenging beliefs that clash with our principles or taking on challenging tasks that others avoid due to their demanding nature. Courage in this context means confronting challenges, but with a thoughtful awareness that growth often emerges from discomfort.

Maintaining a standard also involves acting with integrity in every situation. It is essential to do something even when no one is watching, even if it comes with sacrifices. It involves aligning your actions with your words. For instance, your commitment to preservation should be evident in both your actions, like advocating for sustainable policies, and your personal choices, such as recycling or reducing the use of plastics.

Furthermore, holding yourself to a standard entails showing empathy and serving others. According to Stoicism, humans are beings, and leading a virtuous life means positively impacting other people's lives. Acts of kindness, volunteering, or simply being a reliable friend, coworker, or family member can demonstrate this. High standards are not just about success but also about lifting others up and nurturing a caring community.

Moreover, patience and perseverance play roles in maintaining standards. Personal development is a journey filled with obstacles

The Higher Standard

and difficulties. Stoicism promotes accepting these challenges as part of life and encourages persistence in overcoming them. It's about dedicating yourself to improvement while realizing that perfection may be out of reach, but striving for it is worthwhile.

In summary, upholding oneself to a certain level is a practice in Stoicism that covers various virtues and behaviors. It involves aiming for excellence in character and deeds guided by wisdom, justice, courage, and temperance. This entails being self-aware, disciplined, honest, compassionate, and persistent. Though following standards is demanding, it is also greatly fulfilling, leading to satisfaction and making a meaningful difference in the world. By committing to live up to a standard, one embraces the idea of living well through continual growth and a sense of purpose.

Focus on Correcting Self

"I will focus on judging and correcting my own behavior and not others."

* * *

Stoicism teaches that the only things truly within our control are our own thoughts, actions, and reactions. External events and the behaviors of others fall outside this sphere of direct control. By concentrating on our own behavior, we align with Stoic thought, which advocates focusing energy only on matters within our control. Not only does this lead to more effective personal development, but it also fosters a sense of peace and contentment by preventing constant disturbance from actions beyond our control.

Furthermore, focusing on self-assessment and self-correction is an exercise in cultivating virtue, which Stoics regard as the highest good. Only through introspection and personal action can we truly practice and develop virtues such as wisdom, justice, courage, and temperance. By dedicating ourselves to self-improvement, we strive to live according to these virtues, making decisions that reflect our commitment to a moral life.

Practically implementing this focus begins with regular self-reflection. This involves examining our daily choices and behaviors to assess whether they align with Stoic virtues. For example, at the end of each day, one might reflect on instances where they could have shown more patience or acted more justly. This daily practice not only helps identify areas for improvement but also reinforces positive behaviors.

Self-discipline is crucial in this endeavor. Once we identify aspects of our behavior that need correction, we must exercise self-discipline to make these changes. This might involve setting specific, actionable goals or altering established patterns of behavior that do not serve us well. For instance, if one identifies a tendency to respond hastily to stress, they might commit to taking a few moments to breathe and reflect before reacting to stressful situations in the future.

Moreover, focusing on correcting our own behavior rather than judging others encourages humility—a key Stoic value. Recognizing that we are all works in progress, with our own flaws and strengths, can foster a more compassionate and understanding approach to others. It reminds us that just as we strive and often struggle to better ourselves, so too are others dealing with their own challenges.

Stoicism also teaches the importance of leading by example. By focusing on improving our own behaviors and setting a high standard for ourselves, we can inspire others to embark on their own journeys of self-improvement. This indirect influence can often be more effective than direct criticism or unsolicited advice, as it demonstrates the tangible benefits of a Stoic life.

Additionally, it's important to practice resilience and acceptance. As we focus on our own behavior, we will inevitably encounter failures and setbacks. Stoic resilience means accepting these as part of the journey and using them to learn and grow rather than becoming self-critical or depressed.

Lastly, while Stoics focus on self-improvement, they also recog-

Focus on Correcting Self

nize the value of support and guidance from others. Engaging with a community of like-minded individuals who are also committed to Stoic principles can provide encouragement and insights that further personal growth. Thus, while the focus is on self-correction, it does not mean isolating oneself from the support and wisdom of others.

In conclusion, Stoic philosophy deeply aligns with the commitment to focus on judging and correcting one's own behavior rather than others'. It prioritizes personal responsibility, virtue development, and greater peace and effectiveness. Through regular self-reflection, self-discipline, humility, leading by example, resilience, and community engagement, we can successfully focus on ourselves in a way that not only enhances our own lives but also gently influences those around us. This approach not only fosters personal growth but also contributes to a more virtuous and harmonious society.

Chapter 11
ACCEPTANCE

Facing The Changes

"I understand that life can change in an instance, and I will stand ready to face whatever comes."

* * *

Accepting the unpredictable nature of life enables us to maintain present-moment awareness and eschew the illusion of control over our thoughts and behaviors. This perspective allows us to let go of the stress and unease that arise from attempting to shape every aspect of our lives to fit our desires perfectly. We become adept at navigating life's twists and turns by embracing change and approaching situations with a peaceful mindset. Stoicism instructs us to be mentally prepared for any situation by developing resilience and embracing the moment without anticipating the worst, but emotionally ready to face whatever may come our way.

Reflecting on our thoughts and behaviors can enhance our toughness, enhancing our ability to maintain composure in the face of life's difficulties or obstacles. Practicing mindfulness and being aware of

Becoming Stoic

our reactions to disruptions or surprises in our routines can cultivate a more deliberate approach to adapting to life's fluctuations.

Stoicism also teaches us the importance of preparing for challenging situations so that we're not taken by surprise when they arise. This strategy of "premeditation" entails considering the unpredictability of life's circumstances. We anticipate challenges and strategize our approach ahead of time. We equip ourselves to react with logic and moral integrity rather than with panic or annoyance. Engaging in practice can improve our ability to concentrate on things we can influence despite the circumstances.

It is common to experience feelings of fear or anxiety when unexpected changes occur in life; however, Stoicism suggests that our perception of these events, rather than the events themselves, frequently influences these emotions. For instance, losing a job may appear daunting initially, but philosophy argues that our identity is not determined by our job. What truly counts is the way we decide to react to the circumstance.

Placing an emphasis on virtues such as wisdom and courage, as well as practicing self-control and justice in our actions and decisions as we navigate through life's ups and downs with resilience and honesty. This is the key to staying grounded and true to oneself amidst uncertainties and challenges that come our way.

Then, by embodying these qualities in our actions and mindset, we cultivate a feeling of strength and clarity that remains steady when faced with external challenges. Than succumbing to feelings of dread or doubt, we approach situations with consideration and intent, choosing the most suitable path forward based on our capabilities and constraints.

Stoicism's core principle is the belief that we have power over our thoughts and deeds, but not over circumstances or events that may arise unexpectedly in life's journey. Embracing acceptance doesn't equate to being passive or surrendering; it involves recognizing the truth of a circumstance and opting to react in a manner. When we face a loss or setback we cannot change, we can choose how to move

Facing The Changes

forward. We possess the capacity to learn from events, become stronger as a result, and refocus our focus on our future actions. By embracing the things we cannot change, we liberate ourselves from the upheaval that frequently comes with resisting change.

Stoicism emphasizes that one cannot attain true inner peace by avoiding life's changes. We welcome life's changes with a mindset of preparedness and openness to acceptance. Life is inherently dynamic. Shifts in circumstances and unpredictability will forever characterize life. Nevertheless, by directing our attention towards the aspects within our control—such as our values, our behavior, and our mental outlook—we can discover serenity amidst times.

Once we realize that life can shift suddenly at any moment, we release the desire for everything to unfold precisely as we envisioned. Embracing this realization enables us to live fully in the present, valuing our blessings while recognizing their impermanence. Moreover, it empowers us to develop resilience, assuring us that regardless of circumstances, we possess the fortitude and insight to confront them with bravery and discernment.

Change: The Constant of the Universe

"I acknowledge that everything is constantly changing, and I refuse to attach myself to specific moments."

* * *

Stoicism emphasizes the idea that life is ever-changing and dynamic; things are always shifting beyond our influence or predictability. It suggests that by embracing this reality and not becoming overly attached to moments or results in life's journey, one can discover serenity and steadiness despite the ups and downs of experiences. Change is an aspect of existence, as fluctuations are pervasive in all aspects of our lives—be it relationships, jobs, health, or even our own mental and emotional states. It's natural to desire stability and cling to familiarity or comfort in the moment; however, in Stoicism it is believed that this mindset is not practical as life always progresses forward despite our wishes to hold onto the past.

For instance, experiencing joy when circumstances are favorable is possible. A promotion at work, a friendship, or a period of excellent health are examples. But it's important to remember that these situa-

Becoming Stoic

tions won't stay the same; they might change, promotions could end, and friendships may drift away, and health might deteriorate. Similarly, tough times of sorrow and pain will eventually pass, giving room for experiences. Stoicism teaches us that accepting the nature of everything helps us avoid emotional distress.

We often feel letdown and frustration when we cling to expectations and hopes of permanence and stability in everything we encounter or experience in our lives, ignoring the fact that life is always evolving and shifting around us. This is because things don't stay fixed forever. As an aspect of being human, Stoicism teaches us the importance of accepting and embracing the changing nature of existence, showing us that by acknowledging and adapting to life's fluctuations and uncertainties with grace and resilience rather than resisting or fighting against them, we can navigate through life's twists and turns with more ease and equanimity.

In Stoicism, the concept of attachment refers to tightly holding onto outcomes or people in life, which can lead to unnecessary suffering when things don't go as expected or desired. According to Stoic philosophy, it's crucial to cherish the present moment and value what we have without being excessively attached to it. Being overly attached breeds fear of change loss or unpredictability, inhibiting our ability to live freely and completely.

Consider this scenario: Picture an individual who forms a bond with their job and equates their self-esteem with their career achievements. It is normal to feel a sense of accomplishment in ones endeavors; however, if the circumstances change—like losing the job or encountering a setback—the individual might feel deeply troubled because they have linked their well-being to this factor. Adopting a perspective, on the other hand, would mean finding fulfillment and dedicating oneself to the work without letting it dictate one's self-esteem or happiness. When a person loses or alters their job role and has to adjust, they understand that it's a natural part of life's constant evolution.

This philosophy also holds true in relationships. Stoicism values

Change: The Constant of the Universe

relationships and promotes kindness and fairness towards others, while also recognizing the impermanence of people's nature, like everything else in life undergoes change. Friendships may drift apart or end altogether; loved ones may depart from this world. Relationships can evolve over time. Accepting these transitions enables us to treasure the moments we share with others, free from the overwhelming fear of separation. This mindset facilitates maintaining equilibrium in the face of loss.

One important principle of Stoicism is that embracing change and releasing attachments leads to a sense of freedom. When we refrain from trying to manipulate circumstances outside our influence—like the passage of time or the results of events—we liberate ourselves from stress and concern. This outlook enables us to concentrate on what counts—our thoughts, deeds, and ethical values.

The wisdom of stoic philosophy, which emphasizes the importance of the current moment as the only one within our grasp for influence and control, allows us to live a fulfilling life by not getting caught up in moments of time and fully embracing the present.

This sense of acceptance also aids us in confronting life's obstacles with increased fortitude and perseverance. Knowing that tough times are only fleeting allows us to tackle them with poise and determination, keeping in mind that they will eventually fade away. Similarly, in moments of joy, we can fully enjoy them without worrying about their conclusion.

Detaching oneself doesn't imply turning apathetic or aloof from life; rather, it involves acknowledging the impermanent essence of all things while actively participating in life with intent and sincerity. We can savor moments of joy and accomplishments without grasping onto them. This approach enables us to relish happiness without the shadow of impending loss and confront difficulties without drowning in hopelessness.

In our lives, as humans, we often feel frustrated when things don't unfold as expected or planned out ahead of time. Plans can be fluid and altered at any moment, according to a Stoic perspective. If

Becoming Stoic

we fight against these shifts, we can embrace them. Adjust our course accordingly. When we release our grip from the idea of how things ought to be, we grant ourselves the freedom to react to life's twists and turns in a manner.

When it comes to our aspirations and goals, it's critical to aim for self-improvement and pursue targets. Stoicism emphasizes directing our attention towards the effort we invest rather than fixating on a set outcome. Achieving a desired result may often lie outside our sphere of influence. Our approach to tackling the obstacle remains within reach. By emphasizing the journey over the destination, we can derive satisfaction from our endeavors irrespective of the result.

To sum up, the philosophy of life means recognizing that everything is always evolving and choosing not to hold on to particular moments or results. Embracing life's impermanence helps us release pain and cultivate a sense of tranquility within ourselves. By releasing attachments to outcomes, we can fully embrace life's experiences without fear of change or loss.

Stoicism emphasizes that real liberty stems from our capacity to confront life's uncertainties with wisdom and strength while maintaining composure and dignity throughout the journey of existence by concentrating on managing our thoughts and responses instead of trying to control external circumstances or outcomes. Genuinely embracing each present moment while gracefully releasing it when it fades away leads us toward a harmonious, balanced, and satisfying life.

Accepting Change

"I understand that all things can and will change and completely accept the process."

* * *

Everything in life is in a constant state of flux, from our circumstances to our relationships, and even our own thoughts and emotions. By accepting change as a natural part of life, we free ourselves from unnecessary suffering and learn to live with greater calm and resilience. This perspective helps us to focus on what we can control—our own thoughts and actions—while letting go of our desire to control external events.

One of the central teachings of Stoicism is the idea that nothing remains the same forever. Life is constantly evolving, and everything around us is subject to change. Whether it's the seasons, the stages of life, or the events we experience, change is a natural part of existence. Recognizing this truth allows us to approach life with a more balanced and realistic mindset.

Often, people struggle with change because they hold onto the desire for things to remain stable and predictable. We may want our relationships to stay the same, our health to remain constant, or our jobs to be secure. However, life is full of uncertainties, and things will inevitably shift in ways we cannot always anticipate or control. Stoicism teaches us to embrace this reality rather than fear it. By understanding that change is a fundamental aspect of life, we can prepare ourselves mentally and emotionally to adapt to whatever comes our way.

A key component of accepting change is learning to let go of resistance. Resistance occurs when we cling to the way things were or try to control outcomes that are beyond our reach. This can lead to frustration, anxiety, and stress. For example, if we become attached to a certain way of life—such as a comfortable routine or a specific relationship—we might resist when changes disrupt that comfort. However, Stoicism teaches that resisting change only leads to unnecessary suffering, as it puts us in conflict with the natural flow of life.

We liberate ourselves from this resistance by accepting that change is inevitable. Instead of trying to hold onto the past or control the future, we can focus on living in the present and adapting to whatever life brings. This doesn't mean that we don't care about outcomes or that we give up on our goals, but it means that we approach life with a sense of flexibility and openness. We recognize that while we can influence certain aspects of our lives, we cannot control everything, and that's okay.

Another important aspect of Stoicism is understanding that change is a process, not something that happens instantly or in a single moment. Change unfolds gradually over time, often in ways beyond our immediate comprehension. We should accept this natural process with patience.

For example, personal growth is a type of change that takes time. We may set goals to improve ourselves, whether it's developing a new skill, cultivating a healthier lifestyle, or working on our emotional well-being. However, these changes don't happen overnight. Stoicism teaches us to be patient with ourselves and trust the process, knowing

Accepting Change

that progress takes time. Accepting the gradual nature of change allows us to stay focused on our efforts without becoming frustrated by the pace of progress.

The same principle applies to changes in our external circumstances. Whether it's a career shift, a new relationship, or a transition in life stages, accepting the process of change allows us to approach it with a calm and steady mind. Instead of rushing to the end or becoming anxious about the unknown, we learn to trust that change is a necessary part of life's journey, and that every step of the process brings us closer to growth and new experiences.

A central idea in Stoicism is the importance of focusing on what we can control. We cannot control changes, but we can control our responses. Not stopping change, but adapting and growing in response to it is our true power.

For instance, when faced with a major life transition, such as moving to a new city or starting a new job, we may feel overwhelmed by the uncertainty and unfamiliarity. However, Stoicism encourages us to shift our focus from what we cannot control (the new environment, the reactions of others) to what we can control (our mindset, our actions, and how we choose to approach the situation). By focusing on our own thoughts and behaviors, we become more resilient and better equipped to handle whatever changes come our way.

Acceptance is a powerful tool in Stoicism. When we accept that all things will change, we release ourselves from the anxiety that comes from trying to maintain control over life's uncertainties. Acceptance doesn't mean passivity or resignation—it means recognizing that change is a natural part of life and choosing to face it with courage and grace.

For example, if we face the end of a relationship or the loss of a loved one, Stoicism teaches that while we may feel sadness and grief, we should also accept the impermanence of life. Instead of resisting the reality of change, we can honor the time we had and move forward with the understanding that life is always evolving. This mindset allows us to find peace, even in the midst of loss, because we understand that change is part of the natural cycle of life.

In conclusion, from a Stoic perspective, understanding that all things can and will change—and fully accepting the process—is essential to living a peaceful and resilient life. Stoicism teaches that change is inevitable, and that resisting it only leads to unnecessary suffering. By embracing change and focusing on what we can control—our thoughts, actions, and responses—we can navigate life's uncertainties with greater calm and clarity.

Acceptance of change helps us let go of attachment to specific outcomes and frees us from the need to control everything around us. It allows us to live more fully in the present moment, to grow from our experiences, and to approach life's challenges with a steady and adaptable mindset. Ultimately, by accepting the process of change, we cultivate inner peace and learn to move through life with greater wisdom, strength, and purpose.

Go With the Flow

> "I will accept all events as they are and not struggle against them... flow rather than resist."

* * *

One of the core teachings in Stoicism is that life is unpredictable. Every day, we encounter situations and events that we did not anticipate—some pleasant, some difficult, and some beyond our understanding. These events, whether they involve other people's actions, changes in our environment, or simply the unfolding of life's natural cycles, are often out of our control. The Stoic approach to life teaches that resisting these uncontrollable events only creates unnecessary mental and emotional distress.

When we struggle against events that are beyond our control, we create tension and frustration within ourselves. It's akin to attempting to impede the course of a river; regardless of our exertion, the force of the current surpasses our efforts, leading to our exhaustion. Stoicism teaches that accepting the natural flow of events and adapting to

Becoming Stoic

them is more effective than trying to resist or change the unchangeable.

If we face an unexpected job loss or a sudden illness, our initial reaction might be to resist these changes and wish things were different. We might feel angry, frustrated, or overwhelmed by the situation. However, Stoicism teaches that these feelings of resistance do not change the reality of what has happened. By accepting the situation and focusing on how to respond, we can find peace and be productive.

Acceptance, in Stoic philosophy, is not about giving up or being passive. Instead, it is about recognizing the limits of our control and choosing to focus our energy on what we can influence. Accepting events as they are means acknowledging that life's circumstances are often out of our hands, but our response to those circumstances is always within our control.

When we accept life's events as they unfold, we free ourselves from the mental burden of wishing things were different. This doesn't mean we have to like or enjoy everything that happens; rather, we understand that resisting reality only adds to our suffering. By accepting what is, we can shift our focus from frustration to action —how we can best respond to the situation in a way that aligns with our values and goals.

If a relationship ends unexpectedly, it's natural to feel sadness or disappointment. However, resisting the reality of the situation, wishing it hadn't happened or blaming ourselves or the other person, only prolongs the pain. By accepting the situation, we can initiate the healing process and concentrate on moving forward, instead of lingering on unchangeable aspects. Acceptance allows us to let go of the past and embrace the present moment.

The idea of flowing rather than resisting is central to Stoic thought. New challenges, opportunities, and situations constantly present themselves in life. Stoicism encourages us to flow with these changes, adapting to them with a calm and flexible mindset. Flowing with life is neither passive nor rigid. We can adapt to any situation,

Go With the Flow

making deliberate choices without succumbing to resistance or frustration.

Flowing with life involves recognizing that change is inevitable. We cannot stop time, prevent loss, or avoid difficult situations. However, we can choose how we engage with these changes. By staying flexible and open to life's uncertainties, we become more resilient and better able to handle challenges as they arise.

For instance, we might initially feel anxious or uncertain when faced with a sudden change in our career path. However, instead of resisting the change and wishing things had stayed the same, we can embrace the opportunity for growth. Flowing with the situation might mean learning new skills, exploring different opportunities, or rethinking our long-term goals. Accepting change helps us overcome challenges and thrive.

Resisting life's events often comes from a desire to control outcomes that are beyond our control. We want things to go a certain way, and when they don't, we become frustrated or disappointed. Stoicism teaches that letting go of this resistance is key to finding peace and contentment. By accepting that we can't control everything, we release the tension that comes from trying to force things to go our way.

Letting go of resistance also means letting go of the need for life to be perfect. Life is full of imperfections, setbacks, and difficulties, but these are a natural part of the human experience. Stop resisting life's imperfections and appreciate its beauty and complexity instead of wishing it were different.

Our natural reaction to traffic jams or delays may be frustration or impatience. We resist the situation because it is not what we wanted or expected. However, by letting go of this resistance and accepting the delay as part of life, we can remain calm and focus on what we can control—perhaps using the time to reflect, relax, or listen to a podcast. This shift in perspective allows us to flow with the situation rather than letting it create unnecessary stress.

Ultimately, Stoicism teaches that true peace comes from

Becoming Stoic

accepting life as it is rather than fighting against it. By accepting the events of life and flowing with them, we cultivate a sense of inner calm and resilience. We learn to handle challenges with grace and to find meaning in both the ups and downs of life.

When we stop struggling against what we cannot control, we open ourselves up to the present moment. We become more mindful, more aware, and more capable of responding thoughtfully to whatever life brings our way. This acceptance doesn't mean we give up on improving ourselves or our circumstances; it means we focus our efforts where they can truly make a difference—on our own actions, thoughts, and responses.

Accepting all events as they are and flowing rather than resisting is key to living a life of peace and resilience. While we cannot control life's events, we can control our response, according to Stoicism. We can control our response by letting go of resistance and accepting.

I'll Be Okay

"I will be okay regardless of what happens in my life."

* * *

Stoicism teaches that life is full of uncertainties and challenges, many of which are beyond our control. However, our inner strength, our ability to choose how we think and act, is always within our control. By focusing on what we can control—our thoughts, actions, and attitudes—we can maintain a sense of calm and resilience, no matter what happens in the world around us.

One of the key teachings of Stoicism is the understanding that life is unpredictable. We cannot foresee or control many of the events that will occur in our lives. Situations shift, individuals arrive and depart, triumphs and setbacks transpire, and occasionally we encounter unanticipated challenges. If we overly attach ourselves to the idea of controlling or predicting what will happen, this uncertainty can cause anxiety or fear.

While we cannot control external events, we can control our response, according to Stoicism. The phrase "I will be okay regardless of what happens in my life" reflects this idea. It is an affirmation that, no matter what life throws at us, we have the ability to remain steady and resilient by choosing our mindset and reactions. This sense of inner control is the foundation of Stoic peace.

For example, if we lose a job, face a health challenge, or experience the end of a relationship, it is natural to feel upset or uncertain about the future. Stoicism teaches us to focus on what we can control in these situations. Instead of lamenting the loss or worrying about the future, we can move forward with positivity, knowing that our satisfaction comes from within. By staying grounded in our ability to choose our thoughts and actions, we reassure ourselves that we will be okay, no matter what happens.

Stoicism emphasizes the importance of developing inner strength and self-reliance. Instead of controlling the world, this inner strength controls how we navigate it. Our thoughts, beliefs, and attitudes are the only things we truly have power over, and by focusing on cultivating these inner qualities, we build resilience that allows us to weather any storm.

The belief that our true well-being does not stem from material possessions, external achievements, or the approval of others underpins the statement "I will be okay regardless of what happens in my life." These things are ephemeral and susceptible to loss at any given time. Instead, true well-being comes from living in alignment with our values, acting with wisdom, and maintaining a calm, rational mindset even in the face of adversity.

Someone who loses a significant amount of money in an investment might feel devastated if they had tied their sense of self-worth or happiness to their financial status. However, stoicism teaches that external factors such as wealth do not determine our worth. If we have developed inner strength, we recognize that while losing money may be challenging, it does not define who we are or take away our ability to live a meaningful and virtuous life. By focusing on what we can control—our actions moving forward, our mindset about the situation, and our ability to remain calm—we realize that we can be okay even in the face of financial loss.

A central teaching of Stoicism is the idea of accepting what we cannot control. Life will inevitably bring difficulties—illness, loss, disappointment, and failure—but fighting against these realities or wishing things were different only causes unnecessary suffering. Stoicism encourages us to accept life with all its flaws and uncertainties and focus on how we can best respond.

The mindset of "I will be okay regardless of what happens" is about embracing acceptance. When we accept that many things in life are beyond our control, we free ourselves from the frustration and anxiety that come from trying to change the unchangeable. Acceptance means realizing that we can control our reactions to events, not giving up or being passive.

Stoicism teaches us to accept the reality of a serious illness rather than resisting it. Instead of focusing on fear or frustration, we can focus on how we will respond; by seeking treatment, maintaining a positive attitude, and making the best of each day. Acceptance gives us the power to face challenges with resilience and peace, knowing that our well-being comes from how we choose to engage with life's difficulties, not from avoiding them.

Stoicism also teaches us the importance of perspective. When faced with difficulties, it is simple to get caught up in the moment and feel overwhelmed. However, Stoicism encourages us to step back and view the situation from a broader perspective. Most of our worries and fears may not be as important as they seem. By shifting our perspective, we can reduce the emotional weight of a challenge and remind ourselves that we have the inner strength to handle whatever comes our way.

For example, a missed opportunity or a professional setback may feel like a major loss in the moment, but with perspective, we can recognize that this is just one event in a larger journey. Stoicism teaches us to view these setbacks as temporary and to focus on the long-term growth and learning that can come from them. By main-

Becoming Stoic

taining perspective, we remind ourselves that we will be okay, even if things don't go as planned.

Understanding that our true well-being comes from within underpins the belief that "I will be okay regardless of what happens in my life". Life is full of uncertainties, challenges, and changes, many of which are beyond our control. However, Stoicism teaches that by focusing on what we can control—our thoughts, actions, and responses—we can maintain inner peace and resilience, no matter what life brings. By accepting what we cannot control, developing inner strength, and maintaining perspective, we empower ourselves to navigate life's difficulties with grace and wisdom. This Stoic approach helps us understand that external events do not determine our happiness and peace of mind, but rather our ability to respond to them with calmness and clarity.

Chapter 12
MEDITATION ON MORTALITY

Today Could Be Your Last

"I will strive to live each day as if it were my last."

* * *

Because life is fragile and unpredictable, Stoicism teaches us to appreciate the present moment and not take any day for granted. Living as though each day could be our last encourages us to focus on what truly matters, practice virtue, and let go of distractions and worries that do not serve us. This way of thinking helps us to live more fully and meaningfully.

A key principle in Stoicism is the recognition that life is uncertain and fleeting. We never know how much time we have, and every day could be our last. While this may sound daunting, the Stoic approach is not to live in fear of death, but rather to use this understanding as motivation to make the most of the time we have. Recognizing the fleeting nature of life prompts us to live with purpose, concentration, and immediacy.

When we think about life in this way, we start to appreciate the present moment more deeply. Instead of waiting for some future event to bring us happiness, we realize that every day offers an opportunity to live well. This mindset encourages us to take responsibility for how we spend our time, making sure that we use each day wisely. We don't procrastinate or postpone important decisions, and we don't waste time on trivial matters. Since we may never get another chance, we make the most of our time.

If today were your last day, how would you spend it? This question helps us reflect on what truly matters in life. For many people, the answer would likely involve spending time with loved ones, pursuing meaningful goals, and acting in ways that align with their values. Living each day as if it were your last means prioritizing relationships, actions, and personal growth.

Too often, we lose ourselves in distractions or worries that don't lead to a fulfilling life. We might spend hours stressing over minor inconveniences, or we might pursue goals that don't bring us true satisfaction. Stoicism encourages us to regularly reflect on our priorities and ensure that we are devoting our time and energy to the things that really matter. This might mean letting go of certain distractions, such as constantly seeking approval from others or worrying about things outside of our control.

By focusing on what is essential, we can live each day with a sense of purpose and meaning. Whether it's working toward a personal goal, nurturing relationships, or simply practicing gratitude for what we have, living intentionally allows us to find fulfillment in the present rather than always chasing after some distant future.

Stoicism places a strong emphasis on living a virtuous life. Living each day as if it were your last allows you to act in accordance with your values and virtues—qualities such as wisdom, courage, justice, and self-control. If today were your final day, would you want to act out of anger, selfishness, or fear? Or would you prefer to face the day with kindness, fairness, and strength?

When we focus on living virtuously, we align our actions with our highest principles, regardless of what challenges or opportunities come our way. We can strive to respond with patience and reason in

Today Could Be Your Last

difficult situations, instead of allowing negative emotions to control us. We not only improve ourselves by practicing virtues in our daily lives, but we also contribute to the well-being of others.

Living each day as if it were your last encourages us to treat others with compassion and respect. We don't know how much time we have with the people around us, so it's important to act with kindness and understanding. Whether it's a simple act of generosity or taking the time to listen to someone, these actions are a reflection of the kind of person we want to be.

Living each day as if it were your last also means letting go of regret and fear. Many of us hold onto past mistakes or worry about future uncertainties, but Stoicism teaches that these feelings do not serve us. The past is beyond our control, and the future is uncertain. The only thing we can influence is how we act in the present moment.

By focusing on the present, we free ourselves from the burden of regret and anxiety. Instead of dwelling on what could have been or worrying about what might happen, we take action now. If today were your last day, you wouldn't want to spend it consumed by regrets or fears. Instead, you'd want to focus on making the most of your time and living with courage and mindfulness.

Another aspect of living each day as if it were your last. Stoicism teaches us to value what we have and not take anything for granted. If we knew that today was our last day, we would likely savor every experience—whether it's a conversation with a friend, the beauty of nature, or the satisfaction of completing a task.

Gratitude helps us stay grounded in the present and recognize the value of each moment. It shifts our focus away from what we lack and helps us appreciate the abundance in our lives, no matter how small. By practicing gratitude, we cultivate a sense of contentment and joy that is not dependent on external circumstances.

To live each day as if it were your last means to enjoy the present, act morally, and prioritize what matters. It means living with intention, embracing life's uncertainties, and letting go of distractions,

Today Could Be Your Last

regrets, and fears. Adopting this mindset allows us to live a more meaningful and fulfilling life, aligned with our values and centered around the things that truly bring us happiness. Ultimately, this approach encourages us to live with purpose, gratitude, and presence, making each day count in the best way possible.

What Do You Own?

"I understand that the only thing I truly own are my own thoughts."

* * *

A key Stoic principle is the distinction between what we can and cannot control. Most things in life—our health, wealth, relationships, other people's opinions, and even external events—are largely beyond our control. We can influence these things, but not fully determine their outcome. For example, we can work hard and take care of our health, but unexpected illness may still occur. We can be kind and fair, but we can't control others' reactions.

This realization can be difficult to accept at first because many of us feel a natural desire to control our surroundings and outcomes. We want to achieve success, avoid hardship, and ensure that others treat us well. However, Stoicism teaches that placing our happiness and sense of self-worth in things beyond our control is a path to frustration and disappointment. The world is unpredictable, and if we rely

What Do You Own?

on external factors for our contentment, we are likely to experience anxiety and dissatisfaction when things don't go as planned.

While we cannot control external events, Stoicism teaches that we do have full control over our own thoughts. Our thoughts determine how we perceive the world and how we react to situations. No matter what happens to us, we are empowered to decide how we will think about it. This is the essence of true ownership—unlike external possessions or circumstances, our thoughts are entirely ours to shape and guide.

For example, if we face a difficult situation, such as losing a job or experiencing a personal setback, we cannot change the event itself. However, we can choose how to interpret and respond to it. We can view it as a failure or something that defines our worth, or we can see it as an opportunity to grow, learn, and move forward. By focusing on our thoughts and controlling how we perceive the situation, we can maintain a sense of inner peace, even in challenging times.

This control over our thoughts gives us immense freedom. It means that, no matter what happens in the outside world, we are never completely powerless. We always have the ability to choose how we think, as well as, by extension, how we feel and act. This understanding helps us to live with greater calmness and resilience, as we stop being dependent on things outside of our control for our happiness.

Understanding that our thoughts are the only thing we truly own also encourages us to let go of attachments to external things. We often tie our sense of self-worth and happiness to things outside of ourselves—our possessions, status, success, or relationships. However, Stoicism teaches that these things are fleeting and uncertain. We may lose our wealth, decline in health, or change relationships. If we base our happiness on these external things, we will always be at the mercy of circumstance.

By focusing on our thoughts and not on external attachments, we free ourselves from the emotional ups and downs that come with changes in the outside world. This doesn't mean we stop caring about

What Do You Own?

our lives or the people around us, but rather that we recognize we don't fully control these things. We can appreciate them and work toward our goals, but our inner peace is not dependent on them. This mindset allows us to remain calm and focused, even when life doesn't go as expected.

Stoicism teaches that true freedom comes from within. When we understand that the only thing we truly own is our thoughts, we stop trying to control everything else and focus on what is within our power. This shift in focus leads to a deeper sense of peace because we are no longer weighed down by worries about things we cannot change. We realize that while external events may be uncertain, our thoughts are always within our control, and that gives us the ability to navigate life's challenges with confidence and clarity.

For example, someone who understands this Stoic principle might face a difficult situation, such as criticism from a colleague or an unexpected financial hardship, with a calm and measured response. Instead of reacting impulsively or with frustration, they would reflect on their thoughts, choosing to respond in a way that aligns with their values and maintaining their inner stability. They wouldn't allow an external event to dictate their emotions or derail their peace of mind because they recognize that their response, not the event itself, is what truly matters.

To truly own our thoughts, Stoicism encourages regular reflection and mindfulness. While external events or emotions can easily influence our minds, we can gradually gain more control over our thoughts by practicing self-awareness. This involves noticing when our thoughts are becoming negative or reactive and consciously choosing to shift them toward more constructive, rational perspectives.

For instance, if we find ourselves becoming angry or upset by something beyond our control, we can pause and reflect: "Is this anger helping me? Is it improving the situation?" Stoicism teaches that changing how we think can change how we feel and act. Through

What Do You Own?

this practice, we develop greater mastery over our inner world, which ultimately leads to a more balanced and peaceful life.

While we cannot control external events or other people's actions, we have full power over how we choose to think, interpret, and respond to the world around us. By focusing on what is within our control—our own minds—we can achieve a sense of inner freedom, let go of attachments to external things, and live with greater peace and resilience. Through the practice of controlling our thoughts, we learn to navigate life's challenges with calmness, clarity, and purpose, knowing that our happiness and well-being are ultimately in our own hands.

No Fear

"I will not fear death."

* * *

The Stoics maintain that death is an unavoidable aspect of existence that all creatures must face; thus, worrying about it serves no purpose. Worrying about death prevents us from fully embracing the present moment. Embracing death without fear allows us to lead a life filled with peace of mind and clarity of purpose, according to philosophy. When we release our aversion to death as per Stoicism's teachings and focus on the value of life instead, we can concentrate on what counts in our lives and seize every moment for its potential.

According to Stoic philosophical beliefs, death is an element of the cycle of life. Like birth and aging. It's just a part of life, without positive or negative connotations, but simply an inevitability in nature where everything has its own start and finish, including us humans. Once we come to terms with this understanding, we can see death as something we should not fear or see as abnormal.

The concept of death evokes fear in individuals, as they view it as

No Fear

the end of everything they have known. They experience a world of uncertainty that fills them with dread. Nonetheless, Stoicism advocates redirecting our attention towards manageable aspects of life. Death is part of the cycle; resisting or altering its course is futile. Accepting its certainty enables us to shift our concerns from the future to our actions and existence.

Many individuals are scared of death because of its unpredictability. The uncertainty of what awaits them after death can trigger feelings of anxiety and fear. However, the philosophy of Stoicism advises us not to waste our energy worrying about things that are beyond our comprehension or influence. Instead of dwelling on the mystery of death, the philosophy of Stoicism urges us to focus our attention on the present moment. We concentrate on the present and the choices we make in navigating it.

Stoicism encourages us to live meaningfully in the present by letting go of our worries about the future and fully and freely embracing the moment, rather than dwelling on the unanswerable questions of life after death. When we embrace death as a part of the cycle of life and release ourselves from the weight of fretting about tomorrow's uncertainties, we can then devote our energy to experiencing each moment to its extent.

Once we embrace the notion of mortality without fear holding us back, we can approach life with a sense of direction and understanding. The dread of death frequently guides individuals to choose paths driven more by anxiety than by their values and aspirations. A person gripped by the fear of death might shy away from taking chances, chasing their ambitions, or engaging in challenging activities to maintain a sense of security. Succumbing to fear confines our growth and prevents us from embracing all that life has to offer.

The philosophy of Stoicism emphasizes the importance of living in accordance with our values, letting fear dictate our choices. By acknowledging the inevitability of death and letting go of fear surrounding it, we can prioritize leading a purposeful life focused on kindness and significance. This enables us to make decisions based on

No Fear

our priorities, free from the influence of immediate comfort or fleeting security concerns.

A person who no longer fears death may opt to dedicate their time to fostering connections with others for self-improvement or contributing positively to their lives by engaging in unimportant activities or distractions because they recognize the brevity of life and strive to make the most of it.

Releasing the grip of fear surrounding death enables us to embrace the moment with depth and appreciation. Thoughts of mortality often consume our minds, causing us to overlook the beauty and happiness that surround us in the present moment. Stoicism emphasizes the importance of living in the moment, because it is the time that is truly within our grasp. By directing our attention to the present, we can lead a mindful existence.

When we come to terms with the fact that death's unavoidable, we begin to value life deeply. Every day presents a chance to find significance, be it in sharing moments with those we cherish, pursuing our interests ardently, or relishing in life's joys. Embracing the present allows us to live without remorse, as we understand that we are seizing the moments bestowed upon us.

Stoicism emphasizes the importance of courage as a virtue in life. The ability to confront death without succumbing to fear demands courage, which stems from recognizing that dying is a facet of existence. By embracing death with bravery, it enables us to tackle life's obstacles with a mindset knowingly acknowledging the nature of all things. This viewpoint aids in cultivating resilience, enabling us to navigate challenges with poise and fortitude.

For instance, an individual who has accepted the certainty of death may encounter sickness, grief, or other adversities with a sense of peace, fear, or hopelessness. They understand that these challenges, akin to death, are an inescapable part of life. By fostering bravery, they can confront life's challenges with determination, aware that they possess the fortitude to confront any situation that arises.

Embracing the idea of mortality is not about being apathetic or detached; it's about embracing life with purpose and mindfulness by acknowledging the nature of our existence. Understanding the importance of each day and maximizing our time is key to living a fulfilling life. Whether it involves pursuing a career that matters to us or cherishing moments with loved ones while striving for personal development, awareness of mortality prompts us to lead lives where we prioritize pursuits over trivial distractions.

From a point of view perspective, it concludes that not fearing death helps us lead peaceful and purposeful lives with a sense of fulfillment by embracing death as a natural part of life instead of fearing the uncertainties it brings about. Stoicism guides us to concentrate on the things we can influence. Our choices and values and how we live each day. We shouldn't worry about things that are out of our control, like death. In the end, we find ourselves embracing life with depth and awareness, seizing every moment in its entirety, when we release our grip on the dread of death and embrace it with courage and acceptance.

Motivated Living

"I accept that I can die at any time, which will motivate me to live fully."

* * *

We utilize our understanding of death as a potent drive to lead a purposeful and moral life. Stoicism teaches us to embrace the fact that life is finite, not to inspire fear but to encourage us to make the most of the time we have. By accepting that death can come at any moment, we gain a deeper appreciation for the present, prioritize what truly matters, and learn to live with purpose and intention.

One of life's most fundamental truths is that death is inevitable. No matter how much we may avoid thinking about it, death is a reality that every person will face. Stoicism teaches that rather than fearing death or trying to avoid thoughts of it, we should confront it directly. When we accept that our time on Earth is limited, it changes how we view life. Instead of taking time for granted, we begin to see each day, each moment, as precious.

Instead of dwelling on death in a morbid way, the Stoic approach

Motivated Living

recognizes its certainty, motivating us to live with greater purpose. Understanding that life can end at any time—whether tomorrow, next week, or decades from now—reminds us not to waste our time on trivial matters. Rather, it inspires us to concentrate on what is genuinely significant and lead a life that aligns with our principles.

Accepting that death can strike at any time motivates us to live fully in the present. Often, people get caught up in the distractions of everyday life, worrying about the future or regretting the past. This can lead to a sense of dissatisfaction or feeling that life is slipping by without purpose. However, acknowledging the limited nature of time inspires us to be more present in each moment.

Living fully means appreciating the present for what it is—an opportunity to make meaningful choices, connect with others, and experience life's simple joys. Stoicism teaches that the present is the only time we truly have control over. The past has passed, and the future remains uncertain. By focusing on what we can do right now, we can live with greater intention and mindfulness. This means not waiting for some future event to bring us happiness but finding contentment in the here and now.

For example, instead of postponing meaningful activities or relationships for a future that may never come, we can choose to engage fully with life today. Whether it's spending time with loved ones, pursuing personal growth, or practicing gratitude for what we have, living fully in the present allows us to make the most of each moment.

The awareness of death also helps us clarify our priorities. If we truly accept that life can end at any time, we stop wasting energy on things that do not contribute to our own or others' well-being. Many people spend a considerable deal of time worrying about trivial things —social status, material possessions, or the opinions of others. Stoicism teaches that these external things are not the source of true happiness.

Accepting our mortality encourages us to prioritize living in alignment with our values, cultivating virtues such as wisdom, kind-

Motivated Living

ness, and courage, and positively contributing to the world around us. We understand that we could spend our time more effectively on things that bring lasting fulfillment and meaning, rather than petty arguments, unnecessary stress, or chasing superficial goals.

For example, instead of obsessing over accumulating wealth or status, a Stoic would prioritize spending time with loved ones, pursuing knowledge, or helping others. These are the things that bring true satisfaction and leave a positive impact on the world. We live with a sense of purpose, grounded in the reality of our limited time, when we focus on what matters most.

Accepting death has the key benefit of helping us let go of fear. Many people spend their lives in fear—fear of failure, fear of rejection, fear of loss, and ultimately, fear of death itself. This fear often holds us back from taking risks, pursuing our goals, or fully enjoying life. Stoicism teaches that by accepting death as a natural part of life, we free ourselves from this fear.

We can live more boldly and authentically when we no longer fear death. We stop avoiding challenges or difficult decisions out of fear of the unknown. We live courageously, knowing that while we cannot control our death, we can control how we live until then. This freedom from fear allows us to pursue our dreams, face adversity with resilience, and live with a sense of inner peace.

In Stoicism, accepting death means using it to guide our daily lives, not just preparing for it. Reminding ourselves that life is fleeting inspires us to live a life we would take pride in on our final day. This means acting with integrity, being kind to others, and making choices that reflect our true values.

For example, if today were your last day, would you spend it holding grudges, engaging in arguments, or worrying about trivial things? Or would you prioritize kindness, forgiveness, and purpose? Living each day as if it were our last allows us to live without regret, confident in our ability to make the most of our limited time.

Accepting that we can die at any time is a powerful motivator to live fully and with purpose. Recognizing the inevitability of death

Motivated Living

reminds us to live in the present moment, prioritize what truly matters, and align with our values. The awareness of death helps us let go of fear and distractions, empowering us to live boldly and authentically. Ultimately, by accepting our mortality, we gain the clarity and motivation to live a life of meaning, virtue, and inner peace.

Your Last Day?

"I will remind myself daily that today could be my last day on Earth."

* * *

Instead of instilling fear, contemplating that today might be our day serves as a reminder to live with intention and appreciation for the moment. Stoicism highlights the significance of acknowledging life's nature. Frequently we go about our lives as if time is limitless, assuming that tomorrow or the future will always be within reach. This mindset often results in delaying tasks and failing to appreciate the preciousness of life. Stoicism teaches us to accept the unpredictability of life and the possibility that each day might be our one; by acknowledging this fact and embracing it fully, we can make the most of our time. Live more authentically.

Reflecting upon the possibility that today might be our day compels us to acknowledge the nature of life itself. This insight motivates us to embrace every moment with intention and purpose, instead of delaying crucial choices for an unattainable perfect situa-

Your Last Day?

tion. This way of thinking helps us avoid postponing encounters or connections for the future by acknowledging that there may not always be a "later."

The daily reminder that each day is unique motivates us to live with purpose and mindfulness. When we acknowledge the nature of time, we tend to prioritize what holds true significance in our lives. This entails investing our time in activities that align with our beliefs, bring us joy, and enhance not only our happiness but also that of those around us.

If we were aware that today marked our day on earth, we'd probably choose to surround ourselves with loved ones, indulge in activities that make us happy, and work towards our aspirations. Frivolous matters and pointless disputes would hold no value, as we'd direct our attention to what matters—be it building connections, striving for self-improvement, or supporting a cause close to our hearts.

By embracing the nature of life each day and acknowledging its uncertainties regularly, we cultivate a mindset that encourages us to live with purpose. We no longer allow the days to pass by unnoticed, but instead make decisions about how we use our time. Not only does this mindset shift lead to a more meaningful existence, but it also empowers us to feel a sense of agency over our choices, confident that we are maximizing the moments we have.

Reminding ourselves that today could be our last can be liberating as it allows us to release concerns and anxiety that often consume our thoughts and time for things beyond our control, such as what could happen tomorrow, what others might think of us, or dwelling too much in the past where there's no turning back to change anything. This continuous worrying may hinder us from embracing the moment and experiencing life to its extent.

Stoicism advocates for embracing life's uncertainties and the certainty of death in order to liberate ourselves from nature's anxiety. If today were indeed our day on Earth, would we want to spend it fretting over matters beyond our control? Rather than dwell on the

Your Last Day?

uncontrollable, we would likely prioritize seizing the moment, cherishing the time we have, and maximizing its potential.

Shifting our perspective helps us move away from worrying about the future and appreciate the moment of fearfulness about what's to come. We understand the importance of releasing control over things beyond our power and directing our attention towards what we can influence—our thoughts and behavior. Through this practice, we find calmness. Develop a capacity to face life's obstacles with strength and poise.

It's critical to remember that each day could be our last, and cultivating a sense of gratitude in our lives is equally important! Sometimes, we become so engrossed in the past or the present that we fail to recognize our blessings in the present. We pause to contemplate that today could be our final day here. It serves as a reminder to cherish the present and all the good things that surround us at this moment.

This daily reminder prompts us to express gratitude for the individuals in our lives. We appreciate the opportunities we come across and the minor joys of our daily existence. We relish moments such as sharing a meal with our loved ones, observing a sunset, or simply taking a moment to ponder. We understand the value of cherishing life's simple joys. By being thankful for these moments and experiences in the now rather than always chasing happiness in the future, we can find satisfaction and peace in our circumstances.

For instance, a person who frequently acknowledges the nature of life may consciously show gratitude towards their loved ones who enjoy the beauty of nature or derive happiness from their everyday tasks. By cultivating a sense of thankfulness, we discover a sense of fulfillment and stop ignoring the moments we are fortunate to experience.

Keeping in mind that any given day could be ours also encourages us to live with no remorse or guilt attached to our actions and decisions made in the past. At the end of their lives, a considerable number of individuals find themselves burdened with regrets related

Your Last Day?

to opportunities they didn't seize or connections they didn't prioritize and develop. Stoicism's philosophy guides us in understanding that by acknowledging the nature of life itself, we can steer clear of these kinds of regrets and lead a fulfilled existence.

As if each day could be our last, we act on what matters. We refrain from delaying choices, steer clear of procrastinating our aspirations, and strive to address conflicts or share our emotions. By embracing this approach to life, we can reflect back without remorse, content in the knowledge that we seized the opportunities presented to us.

It's important to remind ourselves every day that today might be our day alive, as it can inspire us to live with meaning and appreciation for what we have in the moment of worrying about things that don't truly matter in the grand scheme of things.

About the Author

Rand Cardwell is a writer, poet, researcher, and lifelong student of Stoic philosophy who has spent over twenty-five years exploring how inner strength is forged through adversity. With a background as a trained military observer and a deep creative sensibility, his work bridges the gap between discipline and reflection. He is the author of several respected books on martial arts, poetry, and philosophy, including the ongoing *Becoming Stoic* series. Cardwell lives in East Tennessee, where he continues to write, reflect, and enjoy the quiet rewards of a deliberate life.

For more books and updates:
www.randcardwell.com

Also by Rand Cardwell

The Western Bubishi

The 36 Deadly Bubishi Points

Unhurried: and other poems

The Becoming Stoic Series

Becoming Stoic: Lessons on Perception

Becoming Stoic: Lessons on Action

Becoming Stoic: Lessons on Will

Becoming Stoic: The Essential Lessons

Cardwell Civil War Series

Brothers in Blue: The Cardwell Men Who Fought for the Union

Brothers in Gray: The Cardwell Men Who Fought for the Confederacy

www.ingramcontent.com/pod-product-compliance
Lightning Source LLC
Chambersburg PA
CBHW071956070526
44583CB00015B/1216